ADVANCE PRAISE FOR

The Literacy Curriculum & Bilingual Education

"Karen Cadiero-Kaplan provides a superb historical analysis of particular ideologies that impact the teaching of literacy. More importantly, the book carefully examines the inextricable relationship between ideology, public policy, and schooling practices, while providing a practical framework for evaluating this relationship within schools. A must read for educators and policymakers who are firmly committed to educational justice for all students."

—*Antonia Darder, Professor of Educational Policy Studies,*
University of Illinois Urbana-Champaign

"Karen Cadiero-Kaplan's far-reaching text invites teachers to critically interrogate and understand their ideological orientations toward marginalized students as well as the instructional practices they utilize with their students. The author provides a detailed historical overview of literacy and bilingual education theories and methods while juxtaposing them with current-day instructional practices. In doing so, she persuades teachers to consciously link their unexamined practices to particular theoretical and ideological schools of thought so as to more clearly understand the ramifications of their practice. Cadiero-Kaplan comprehensively and critically weaves together various bodies of literature with her own ethnographic classroom research in order to model for teachers what it means to struggle to become a coherent, critical, and ideologically clear educator."

—*Lilia I. Bartolomé, Associate Professor of Applied Linguistics,*
University of Massachusetts Boston

The Literacy Curriculum & Bilingual Education

Studies in the
Postmodern Theory of Education

Joe L. Kincheloe and Shirley R. Steinberg
General Editors

Vol. 243

PETER LANG
New York • Washington, D.C./Baltimore • Bern
Frankfurt am Main • Berlin • Brussels • Vienna • Oxford

Karen Cadiero-Kaplan

The Literacy Curriculum & Bilingual Education

A Critical Examination

PETER LANG
New York • Washington, D.C./Baltimore • Bern
Frankfurt am Main • Berlin • Brussels • Vienna • Oxford

Library of Congress Cataloging-in-Publication Data

Cadiero-Kaplan, Karen.
The literacy curriculum and bilingual education:
a critical examination / Karen Cadiero-Kaplan.
p. cm. — (Counterpoints; vol. 243)
Includes bibliographical references and index.
1. Literacy—Social aspects—United States. 2. Education,
Bilingual—Curricula—Social aspects—United States. 3. English
language—Study and teaching—Foreign speakers—Social aspects—United
States. I. Title. II. Counterpoints (New York, N.Y.); v. 243.
LC151.C33   302.2'244—dc21   2003012145
ISBN 978-0-8204-6715-3
ISSN 1058-1634

Bibliographic information published by **Die Deutsche Bibliothek**.
Die Deutsche Bibliothek lists this publication in the "Deutsche
Nationalbibliografie"; detailed bibliographic data is available
on the Internet at http://dnb.ddb.de/.

Cover art: "Transformation" by Carmen E. Quintana
Cover design by Sophie Boorsch Appel

The paper in this book meets the guidelines for permanence and durability
of the Committee on Production Guidelines for Book Longevity
of the Council of Library Resources.

To my late father, Emanuel J. Cadiero, whose spirit and passion for life and learning through dialogue with people is always with me. To my mother, Theresa English, who taught me how to be a strong and independent woman, to believe in myself and to follow my dreams.

Table of Contents

Foreword

Peter McLaren
Professor, UCLA

At the time of this writing the United States is engaged in a shameful and egregious attempt to characterize its imperialist aggression against "failed nation states"—at this current historical moment that country happens to be Iraq—as an intervention on behalf of and in the pursuit of democracy. Under the banner of freedom (meaning the free market), the United States has unleashed a preemptive hell against a cruel and brutal regime allegedly in order to save the lives of Iraqi citizens from a dictator and to save the world from his weapons of mass destruction, while at the same time gaining control of the second–largest oil reserves on the planet and securing the most lucrative contracts to rebuild a country it will have devastated twice in just over a decade. But this banner of freedom has grown faded, its once–shimmering material worn to a threadbare transparency. Its former luster has been reduced to the coat of grease on the shiny "freedom fries" that are currently on sale in the cafeterias of Congress.

Fewer nations now cheer the almost certain victories that follow in the wake of freedom's most powerful phallomilitary warriors. Increasing numbers of the world's poor and oppressed have grown to fear the sound of democracy's arrival: the gunships hovering overhead, the screams of those instantly dismembered by "shock and awe," the wailings of the survivors, the suitcases of cash handed over to government officials as part of the negotiations, and payoffs to the bankers and politicians that few can refuse. If the bribes don't work, the threats are so ominous that nation after nation will likely tumble like a row of dominoes. To bring about democracy isn't an easy business. It's become both a Herculean and imperial task, worthy of the Roman gods, for it will take an empire to accomplish the mission and the vast power of a mighty military machine to achieve and sustain the victory. In the case of Iraq, it has taken relentless bombing, a decade of sanctions that amounted to genocide, and ongoing diplomacy at the point of a gun. It's still too early to tell what the consequences will be, but in the meantime our homeland leaders are telling us to sit back and enjoy the victory. Beer and chips anyone? With the electronic and ink-splotched tentacles of the corporate media reaching into the living rooms of so many homes, is it any wonder that millions of viewers remain helplessly in the thrall of the greatest propaganda force known to humankind: American newspapers, television, and radio shows, the vast majority of them seemingly championing the voices of freedom while at the same time reproducing the ruling ideology that teaches us to enslave ourselves to the rule of capital. Never has the central insight of Marx—that the ruling ideas are the ideas of the ruling class—been more appropriate than these days of full-spectrum media saturation. Often placing a sublime façade over a cruel reality, the media manage the conflict between what is apparent and what is real, its smoke and mirrors fashioning what is true and what is false with a power unimaginable even a century ago.

Enter Karen Cadiero-Kaplan and her new book, *The Literacy Curriculum & Bilingual Education: A Critical Examination. A critical educator,* Cadiero-Kaplan's key concern is the teaching of literacy in a way that both invites and enables students to understand and act upon the ideological ramifications of their received knowledge and to provide students with the opportunity to reflect on their beliefs and practices. This is not the type of literacy that will bode well for the state organs of official ideology because it is essentially an approach to literacy that not only strikes fear into the hearts of the entrenched fanatics of empire-building, but also speaks to the hearts and minds of combatants for popular democracy, who can often be found in the embattled communities of color that are trying to define themselves in opposition to, and defend themselves against, the ruling ideology and social practices. This is because the author is able to link knowledge to power, and pedagogy to the struggle of aggrieved communities against oppression.

This book is also about teachers who are struggling to become more effective practitioners in their work with immigrant and language minority students. With this in mind, Cadiero-Kaplan adopts a premise central to the critical tradition—that literacy is constructed socially as part of the process of reading the word and the world—and charts out a typology of four common ideologies of literacy: functional literacy, cultural literacy, progressive literacy, and critical literacy. This sets the stage in the book for an important historical analysis of how literacy policy is reflected in bilingual education policies, and the author importantly focuses the discussion on California's infamous Propositions 187 and 227. Especially crucial here is the author's discussion of the pervasively dismissive period of bilingual education in which we now find ourselves, where the learning of a majority second language functions to undermine a student's first language and culture, thus creating what is essentially a subtractive situation. We are witnessing the shocking dismantling of bilingual programs throughout the country, where we watch dumbstruck as they are replaced with a compensatory education model of structured English immersion. Cadiero-Kaplan despairs that other states, including Arizona and more recently Massachusetts (the site of the first public mandated bilingual education programs in the country), are even adopting more restrictive measures than Proposition 227.

After providing us with a useful and creative framework for identifying and analyzing language policy along ideological and historical positions, the author invites us to consider two central concepts of critical theory: the historicity of knowledge and hegemony. This helps the reader in Cadiero-Kaplan's important discussion of critical pedagogy, where she emphasizes historic-ideological aspects of knowledge production. Knowledge production, as the author so perceptively understands, is central to dialogue, and to enabling students to reflect critically on their lived realities and experiences. Recognizing that the literacy forms valued and valorized in schools may not adequately reflect the forms of literacy that are prevalent within the culture, community, or home of the students, Cadiero-Kaplan sets forth a number of literacy strategies: oral literacy, signature literacy, recitation literacy, decoding/analytic, and new standard approaches. She concludes with a perceptive analysis of institutional practices and effects of literacy ideologies, calling for a deeper understanding of the political structures that support the oppressive practices under-girded by racist, sexist, and class-biased concepts of knowledge and ability. The pedagogy advanced by the author is both critical and dialogical, giving a central place to generating knowledge through critical praxis, and offering a definition of liberation that is both concrete and dialectical.

The Literacy Curriculum & Bilingual Education is a book that deserves to be engaged by new generations of teachers and teacher educators who understand the political ramifications of living in a society where large numbers of citizens are either unwilling or unable to challenge the dominant knowledge systems that make and remake us in our everyday lives. The hope of building a world in which the public can play a more critical role in challenging systems of domination rests with educators such as Karen Cadiero-Kaplan and others like her.

Peter McLaren
Professor, University of California, Los Angeles

Acknowledgments

This book is the result of a journey that began a lifetime ago and emerged into a research agenda seven years ago. As with any journey one embarks upon in life there are signposts, guides, and friends along the road who contribute, challenge, embrace, and question the path you are on. Some distract, and others push you further than you ever imagined you could go. They contribute their experiences, ideas, and values, and beliefs, when you are tired, unsure, and overwhelmed. However, all these people make the journey more real and fulfilling. To this end, I am grateful to those who surrounded me and joined me on this road.

I begin by acknowledging all those whom I have worked with as teachers in public schools, my many elementary and high school students who taught me more than they will ever know, and to my colleagues in my doctoral program. All of these people who cannot be named specifically are important for they were travelers with me throughout the years, and helped me define my path at a time when I wasn't always confident where I was headed. To all of you I owe my deepest gratitude and respect.

I also have many knowledgeable and caring guides, including Ruben Espinosa, a longtime friend and mentor who shared with me maps, metaphors, and many stories that enabled me to confront my fears by looking at them in a new light; Alberto Ochoa who taught me the importance of following my passion and is always pushing me to go further; and Sally Thomas who guided me to the key readings, ideas, and pedagogy for literacy and reading, the elements that became signposts for my emerging framework. And when I thought I could not possibly go on, there appeared my spirit guide, Antonia Darder, who introduced me to critical pedagogy and the politics of difference. She touched my heart and spirit. Antonia graciously honored my successes and challenged me to go further than I could see. She was and is always there to listen, question, and share her wisdom and passion. It is her work and model that propels me to push further, always. Once the framework was established I encountered more people on the road. Most important were the inspirational and dedicated teachers, without whom this work would not have been possible. I am grateful to the many teachers who took the time to share their stories of struggle and hope, and their literacy beliefs, values and practices.

My heartfelt thanks to Patricia Hinchey for reading an early draft of my work and guiding me in the process of sharing it with the editors of Peter Lang. I am grateful to my editors, Shirley Steinberg and Joe Kincheloe, for their responsive feedback and for providing me with the opportunity to publish this work and put it out into the larger world. I thank Peter McLaren for his support and, after reading my manuscript, addressing the text's themes in the current historical and sociopolitical context. All journeys are situated within a particular space and time, and I appreciate his words of reflection and critique of this historical moment in the context of literacy. I owe a special debt of thanks to Martha Pedroza for her loving patience in guiding me through the world of publishing, and for taking great care in typesetting and formatting this text and reminding me to move slowly. I am also grateful to the production personnel at Peter Lang; Sophie Appel and Phyllis Korper, for keeping me on track and being there to answer all my questions.

My travels would not have been possible or complete without the love and support of my family and friends, who never fail to bring me back home when I need to pause and breathe in the world. I owe a special thanks to my comadres Antonella Cortese and Susie Marks Watt, for reading, rereading, and editing my early drafts, and for being there with a kind heart and open ear whenever I called. A special thanks to my niece Stephanie Cadiero who never failed to reminde me when it was time to work and sometimes to play. Most importantly, I owe my deepest gratitude to my husband and partner in life, Roger Kaplan, who has always believed in me and whose patient spirit and love nurtures and encourages all my adventures in work and life.

Lastly, gracias especialmente a mi querida comadre, Carmen E. Quintana for creating the artwork, Transformation, that graces the cover of this text. I appreciate and value Carmen's friendship, creativity, and work in bilingual education, and share with you her description of her painting titled Transformation.

Transformation has taken root when you have undergone such a change in your life; spiritual, religious, political, educational, and/or philosophical, that you can no longer return to what you were before the transformation took place. The image of the apple and the orange symbolize transformation. The apple in the background is painted orange. If you were to cut it open, it would be an apple. This symbolizes that if you, as a person, change only on the outside but remain the same on the inside, you have not transformed. That is only false change. The apple in the foreground is painted red, however, the inside is an orange. If you taste it, you will taste an orange. When you have changed how you believe, how you feel, look and act, to a point where you can never be what you once were, you have transformed.

In education, transformation must include a hope that all who work with children and community will come together as educational warriors and commit to social justice for all and to a new peace for a better humanity.

The following copyright holders are gratefully acknowledged for granting permission to reprint:

Cadiero-Kaplan, K (2002). *Literacy Ideologies: Critically Engaging the Language Arts Curriculum. Language Arts Journal* 79 (5), 372-392. Copyright 2002, by the National Council of Teachers of English. Reprinted with permission.

M. E. Brisk (1998) *Bilingual Education: From Compensatory to Quality Schooling* (p. xix), Mahwah, NJ: Lawrence Erlbaum Associates. Copyright 1998 by Lawrence Erlbaum Associates, Inc. Reprinted with permission.

Introduction

Reading the world always precedes reading the word, and reading the word implies continually reading the world ... this movement from the word to the world is always present; even the spoken word flows from our reading of the world. In a way however, we can go further and say that reading the word is not preceded merely by reading the world, but by a certain form of writing it or rewriting it, that is, of transforming it by means of conscious, practical work. For me, this dynamic movement is central to the literacy process (Freire & Macedo, 1987, p. 35).

It wasn't until I read Paulo Freire's work that I understood that the struggle I had in school (and that many of my students had in learning to read and write) was a result of learning the word as separate from the world. As a high school student I was tracked as being a poor reader and therefore received a curriculum that focused on teaching me the skills of reading the word. My unique effort to decode and comprehend texts was measured by tests that repeatedly determined that I needed more skills instruction. Later, as a high school teacher of language minority students and students with learning disabilities, I was provided with similar skills-based materials, curriculum, and processes that were designed to help my students become literate in English or bring them up to grade level in reading. Similar to my own high school experience, my students were being asked to learn to read and write, reading the word but not the world, and subsequently being tracked into the system as underachievers.

As a classroom teacher, I did not feel that the teaching methods and materials based on research by experts and touted as the best approach for teaching literacy reflected my experiences in the classroom. That is, the processes and materials that helped my students learn and become literate, (my best practices) were determined by my students and myself. I didn't see a direct connection between theory and practice, between the word and my world. It was from this perspective that I began my own research.

This book and the research it is based on came from my own need, as a classroom teacher, to discover how literacy is defined, by whom, and for what purposes. I wanted to know why curriculum methods for teaching reading changed like the seasons. As an elementary school teacher, I found that in some years, skill instruction was the most appropriate method, while in other years whole-language instruction was more useful.

In the 1980s, as a special education teacher, we were told to throw away our phonics reading programs, which are based on decoding and analyzing, and replace them with a new whole-language program that advocated the use of authentic literature. When I asked why teachers couldn't use both programs, I was informed that the new program was better. Along with other teachers, I challenged the administration at that time and received approval to use both, but with certain stipulations. Contradictions such as these provoked me to search for a more reasonable, realistic, and accurate measure of "best" approaches. The goal of my research was to engage teachers of English language learners (ELLs) in real conversations about their beliefs regarding these educational policies, in order to make a connection between theory and practice and to build a bridge between the world of teachers and the word of research.

This book reflects the work of articulating and synthesizing the research literature on literacy education, bilingual education, and the politics and ideology that inform both. However, connecting policy alone without engaging classroom practice would be a mistake, so the last part of this text highlights the beliefs and practices of teachers, and throughout the text each reader will have an opportunity to reflect on his/her own beliefs and practices. It is only through such reflective processes that teachers and educators can begin making a connection between ideology, politics, pedagogy, and teacher practice.

This introduction describes the significance of this investigation, defines literacy and ideology as they will be considered in this text, and provides an overview of the conceptual framework that not only informs this work, but provides a tool for analyzing policy and programming for literacy instruction in the school context.

It is important to consider the population of students that were the impetus for my research—high school English language learners who arrive in our schools from other countries on a daily basis or are born here and live in communities that speak a language other than English and have received the majority of their schooling here. In 1987 this population of students accounted for 12% of the total K–12 enrollment in the state of California; by 1997 this had increased to 24.5%. By the year 2030, ELLs will represent 70% of the total student population (Garcia, 1993). Furthermore, Los Angeles, Orange, and San Diego counties accounted for more than 57% of the statewide ELL enrollment (California Consortium for Teacher Development, 1997). Historically, California state policy for immigrant and language minority students has focused on elementary school programs. This emphasis is understandable, as there have traditionally been more limited English proficient (LEP) students in elementary schools than in secondary schools, but the number of LEP students in secondary schools has been growing rapidly. In 1987, LEP students enrolled in grades 7–12 in the state totaled 181,442; by 1990 that number had grown to 260,398 (or almost one-third of the state's LEP population), and today the enrollment is up to 489,719 LEP students in grades 7–12, (California Department of Education, 2002).

There has been limited research in this area, a fact supported by a review of 33 studies on effective schools and classrooms for ELLs, only 9 of which focused on middle and high school populations (August and Hakuta, 1997). One reason for this disparity in research is the assumption that students at the secondary level have already received the necessary literacy instruction, so for them instruction becomes focused on content area skills (i.e., science, math), rather than the development of English literacy (Garcia et al., 1995). Although the key component for increasing academic achievement for English language learners is through language development (Chamot, 1998), a focus solely on language development can be problematic without considering literacy in all of its forms, processes, and ideologies; an area rarely examined in school contexts. In the research volume *So Much to Say: Adolescents, Bilingualism & ESL in the Secondary School*, Faltis (1999) states that researchers and educators concerned with this population need to consider three issues: first, knowing who their students are; second, understanding the curriculum and how its dimensions should be adjusted to meet the needs of the students; and third, an awareness and understanding of the "political, structural, and pedagogical issues that interact with contextual considerations at secondary school sites across the nation" (p. 2). To this end, how many teachers in real schools with large populations of ELLs have the opportunity to discuss curriculum beyond the immediate needs of the students and increasing academic demands?

In response to these issues I advocate broadening the scope of concern for all grade levels and all students. All too often texts and research meant for teachers deal with literacy and language development that concerns particular grade levels, ages, abilities, or programs. This book not only adds to the limited research base on secondary programming for immigrant and language minority students, but more importantly provides a tool for all teachers and teacher educators who are interested in literacy and language development, to use in critically examining their beliefs and practices and improving their teaching and learning processes. The latter is accomplished through understanding, from both a historical and ideological perspective, the definitions and processes of literacy instruction, the literacy curriculum, and the resulting programs that are present in our schools.

To begin, I define ideology as the beliefs and views we hold of the world and its reality that are derived from our lived experiences and the most commonly accepted view of the world in which we live and work (Galindo, 1997). Ideology then challenges us to consider the positioning of all points of view, even those accepted to be the most common or appropriate. The ideology that informs my definition of literacy is stated best by Auerbach (1991):

> There can be no disinterested, objective, and value-free definition of literacy: The way literacy is viewed and taught is always and inevitably ideological. All theories of literacy and all literacy pedagogies are framed in systems of values and beliefs which imply particular views of the social order and use literacy to position people socially (p. 71).

This quote in relation to my definition of ideology contends that any definition of literacy is inherently connected not only to pedagogical beliefs and our views of how students learn to read and write, but also to personal and societal values and norms as well. So it could also be stated that those whose definition of literacy is inconsistent with the dominant or accepted view would most likely hold a counter ideological view. Such issues related to literacy and ideology become most important to consider today as the number of immigrant students and English language learners increases, schools nationally focus on testing discrete knowledge skills, and the public reacts in various ways to the increasing diversity of our population. The most recent public reactions include passage of ballot initiatives entitled "English for the Children" beginning with Proposition 227 in California in 1998, Proposition 203 in Arizona in 2001, and most recently, in 2002, voters in Massachusetts responded overwhelmingly, passing a measure that eliminated bilingual education programs across the state. These measures overtly emphasize the importance of English literacy, with literacy defined in very narrow, skill-based terms, and further position English as a national language, thus negating the role that primary language and various forms of literacy have in student learning.

Such ideological hegemony is further perpetuated through the construction of standardized assessments that reflect a standard form of English (Apple, 1995). Such struggles exist due to contradictions in the system as reflected in policies such as Prop. 227, which perpetuates racial and ethnic stereotypes and in doing so, places English and minority languages in opposition to each other. Such contradictions then force suppressed and oppressed individuals and groups to react to rules, impositions, and curriculum standards reproducing "types of personal development compatible with the relationship of dominance and subordination in the economic sphere" (Bowles & Gintes, 1976, p. 11). To begin to understand the context of literacy instruction within education, it is important to clarify how varying perspectives or definitions of literacy reflect different ideologies. Chapter 1 of this text provides definitions of the ideologies of functional, cultural, progressive, and critical literacy, which are connected to public policies for literacy and bilingual education in Chapter 2, thus positioning these policies and ideologies in a historical context.

Part II of this text will examine more fully the connections among ideology, policy, pedagogy, and practice. The critical analysis of literacy and policy within this work is meant to engage readers in dialogue and reflection on curriculum ideology and practice. For, it is only through a thorough understanding of the ideological connections to the history of the literacy curriculum and bilingual education that educational researchers and leaders can begin to address the cultural hegemony that has been, and is, a constant affront to the linguistic, social, cultural, and community consciousness that in large part underlies group antagonisms. Normative assumptions about what it means to be literate, without critical dialogue and reflection, further legitimize an ideological perspective of literacy that is a skill "acquired by an individual, generally within an educational context, utilizing oral language as a basis and ultimately affecting cognitive development" (McKay, 1993, p. 8). Such a position on literacy is necessary, but as this text will make clear, it cannot be the only approach taken by teachers of English language learners. As Brisk and Harrington (2000) state:

> Bilingual students who are perfectly fluent in English are different from native speakers of English who do not know another language or have not experienced another culture. The additional and different knowledge they bring to school must be considered in the teachers' perspective of the students, teaching strategies, and curricular considerations (p. 1).

The intent here is to bring to the forefront the ideas, beliefs, perspectives, and the sociocultural contexts of the students with whom we work, and the schools and society in which we teach and live, while revealing the narrow view of literacy most school literacy curricula currently advocate that promote skills based reading methods of decoding and comprehension measured by discrete skill tests. Such programs and policies are defined by recent educational policies such as NCLB (No Child Left Behind) Reading First initiative. This federal policy advocates institutional and societal contexts for literacy that are more homogenized through use of language and literacy programs that are dictated by very specific and narrow ideological and political perspectives. The result reflects the cultural hegemony that becomes known as "legitimate knowledge." I believe that in order for teachers to be able to critically examine the policy and resulting educational responses they need a framework where educational processes and pedagogy are presented to guide dialogue, foster questions, and promote reflection—not dictate it.

Language Policy and Programming: A Conceptual Framework

Only through communication can human life hold meaning. The teacher's thinking is authenticated only by the authenticity of the students' thinking (Freire, 1993, p. 58).

In his paper *Language Wars: The Ideological Dimensions of the Debates on Bilingual Education*, Rene Galindo (1997) states that "the debates over the future of bilingual education call for conceptual frameworks that can illuminate the variety of issues that are implicated in those debates" (p. 103). The research framework presented here not only addresses this call, but provides crucial reflective processes that can support further dialogue and understanding of teaching practices and curriculum for all immigrant and language minority students.

As can be seen in the Language Policy & Programming Conceptual Framework, depicted in Figure 1, multiple issues of policy and programming are addressed. The framework is designed to analyze policy and programming for ELLs in schools at both macro and micro levels. The Policy for ELLs is the macro level, which can be examined from any one of the multiple policy levels; School Site Program Components is the micro level, ranging from administration to students and parents. As the model illustrates, both Policy and School Site Program elements are then analyzed across six dimensions. The six dimensions of analysis include:

- *Value for Learners:* This area examines how ELLs are viewed within the policies and programs in which they participate, and how they are perceived by concerned stakeholders (i.e., teachers, administrators, parents, self). Areas of concentration include identifying how students' are valued as participants in the learning process, and how they are valued for being bilingual, biliterate, or learning English.

- *Literacy Orientation:* This area examines the various definitions of literacy among stakeholders. Areas of concern here include the value that is placed on literacy as well as recognition for various forms of literacy and language learning—essentially how literacy is valued, not only among teachers and students but across policies and programs. This dimension seeks to clarify the multiple forms of literacy that are important and/or valued by stakeholders.

- *Instructional Goals:* This area identifies the goals of instruction and learning, including expectations of the learner with respect to learning English and content area literacy.

- *Resources:* This domain is concerned with the financial, material, and human resources that are allocated/dedicated to programming and curricula for ELLs. Included here are personnel resources such as the capacity of the teaching staff and materials utilized in curriculum development and teaching.

- *Accountability and Assessment:* This domain seeks to determine accountability of not only student achievement and success, but also program implementation including transition and testing, and the levels of accountability of those responsible for the process.

- *Expectations for Learners:* On this level the framework seeks to clarify expectations of students as defined by the stakeholders, policies, and programs. For example, by graduation, what are students expected to be able to do and/or accomplish, including expectations and methods of preparedness.

These six dimensions are further cycled through the varying program models schools implement to address the needs of English language learners.

Program Approaches: This dimension examines the multiple programs presently utilized or engaged within classrooms and schools. Program models most often found at the secondary level include: Specially Designed Academic Instruction in English (SDAIE), English as a Second Language (ESL, also called English Language Development or ELD), and transitional bilingual models. Each program approach can then be evaluated across the six dimensions above. The core concern here is, how does program approach support or interact with literacy orientation, instructional goals, resources, accountability/assessment, and expectations for learners?

Figure 1: Language Policy and Programming
Conceptual Framework

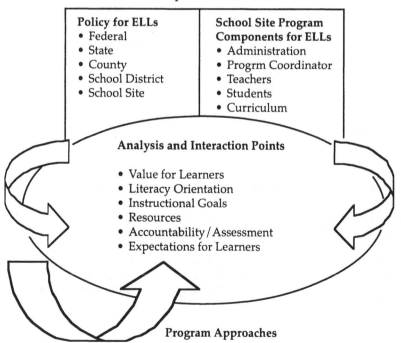

Policy for ELLs
- Federal
- State
- County
- School District
- School Site

School Site Program Components for ELLs
- Administration
- Progrm Coordinator
- Teachers
- Students
- Curriculum

Analysis and Interaction Points

- Value for Learners
- Literacy Orientation
- Instructional Goals
- Resources
- Accountability/Assessment
- Expectations for Learners

Program Approaches

To actualize this conceptual model in practice the Program Evaluation Instrument (Table 5) was developed. This instrument is utilized to evaluate the six elements defined above, which impact student learning and success. While the instrument was initially designed and utilized to examine programming for ELLs (Cadiero-Kaplan, 2001), it can also be utilized to examine policy and programming elements for any school population or program. The purpose of including both the conceptual and working framework is to provide the reader with a representation of the levels in which both policy and programming are engaged within and across all levels of the school system. However, in order to utilize this instrument for program evaluation it is necessary to first understand varying definitions of literacy, the role ideology plays in our engagement of policy and programs, and the curriculum programs that result.

This book will address these issues by examining critically the connection between literacy ideologies, politics, and teacher practice. Here teacher practice includes the pedagogical and curricula decisions that may foster or impede literacy development for students. The intention is not only to identify and define literacy from a policy perspective, but to question what we do as educators and teachers, and further ask how, why, and with whom we take up curriculum and teaching practices (Walsh, 1996). Therefore, the conceptual framework presented and this text are positioned within a critical pedagogical approach that necessitates a

> thoughtful consideration of our individual perspectives and positions including how they came to be, as well as a thoughtful consideration of our pedagogy and practice in and out of the classroom. Such a process requires that as educators, we become more cognizant of the differences between our students and ourselves—racial, ethnic, cultural, economic, residential, and generational (growing up in today's world vs. when we were children)—of the overt and hidden ways that some students' voices are trivialized and denied, and of the ways that the policies, relations, and instructional, and language practices of our classrooms and school reproduce the power and ideology of the broader society (Walsh, 1996, pp. 227–228).

It is from this critical perspective that Chapter 1 illustrates and articulates the functional, cultural, progressive, and critical ideologies of literacy. Chapter 2 takes this analysis further by historically linking ideologies of literacy to public policies on literacy and bilingual education from the 1600s to the present. Chapter 3 examines how our own histories inform our perceptions and beliefs, how curriculum is defined in schools, and considers the hegemonic factors of the literacy curriculum. So, while Part I provides the theoretical foundation of literacy ideologies as they relate to public policy literacy, Part II reflects on teacher practice and processes that are derived from these ideologies and policies. To begin this process, Chapter 4 reframes both literacy ideology and forms of public policy for literacy within teacher pedagogy and practice. Chapter 5 illustrates how the ideologies of functional/cultural and progressive/critical are engaged in school settings. The final chapter provides the reader with a process for undertaking his/her own interrogation of jis/her beliefs and practices of literacy and those of the curriculum presently promoted within schools.

Since I believe it is necessary for teachers to not only understand theory, but also to enact it and make a connection between theoretical models and beliefs and practice, I have included in each chapter of this text a reflective activity. These activities are designed to engage the reader in the process of reflection and dialogue. Such activities are based on a critical action research approach, one that requires "a 'first-person' perspective in which people construct the research process as a way of collaborating in the process of transforming their practices, their understanding of their practices, and the situation in which they practice" (Kemmis and Wilkson, 1998, p. 32). It is my hope that readers of this text will take up this work in dialogue, debate, and discussion with peers and mentors, and as a result "attempt not to simply understand or describe the world of practice but to change it" (Kincheloe 1995, p. 77). Change cannot, however, be imposed by a researcher or author because the participants, or readers in this case, undertake critical changes in this process partly due to the fact that they have chosen to reflect on and improve their practice (Cochran-Smith & Lytle, 1993).

Whether you chose to do this or not, I encourage you to consider that it is only through critical dialogue that we can begin to consider our own historical positions, and to engage dialectically our ideologies and those of the educational spaces within which we function daily. Thus, critical literacy challenges us to broaden our conceptions of how we actively produce, sustain, and legitimate meaning and experience in our classrooms' main issues that this text is designed to engage (Freire & Macedo, 1987). However, practically I have to be aware that just raising the contradictions or tensions that are part of our professional experiences can be "insufficient unless it is also supplemented by an awareness of the ideological construction of our consciousness and the education and political results of such construction" (Kincheloe, 1995, p. 81). To this end, I challenge readers to take up true praxis by keeping a journal as you read this text, responding to all the reflective activities, and most importantly, reflecting and acting on feedback from peers, professors, and your own children and students about your beliefs and their beliefs about literacy and classroom practice.

This approach to teacher development is not new, as Dewey (1904) advocated it in his writings; in order for teachers to develop and refine practice they need to be "adequately moved by their own ideas and intelligence" (p. 16). To this end we must realize that we as teachers and educators are both consumers and producers of knowledge about teaching, learning and classroom life. This dialogical approach is based on Freire's belief that the process of knowing or knowledge is a relational act, where "knowledge is not merely produced in the heads of experts, curriculum specialists, school administrators, and teachers, but is informed through the social and cultural conditions that contribute to the forms of knowledge and meaning that students bring to school" (Freire & Macedo, 1987, p. 15). So it is both necessary and imperative for us to examine the interest and principles of those who teach and the curriculum and policies that inform resulting educational practice—a practice that ultimately impacts the literacy development of the children, adolescents, and adults we teach. If such praxis or action is not taken, we run the risk of allowing policy to dictate the curriculum for literacy development and the definitions of best practice. This is not a risk I am willing to take.

Part 1
School Curriculum:
Ideology & Politics of Literacy
& Bilingual Education

This part of the text is comprised of three chapters. They describe and examine the manner in which the school curriculum and literate knowledge become "legitimatized" in schools. This examination of the historical context of literacy curricula reveals how textbooks, reading materials, and instruction function in supporting specific political and ideological agendas and make certain knowledge "legitimate" while appropriating certain literacies in order to perpetuate and sustain societal distinctions based on race and class (Freire & Macedo, 1987; Myers, 1996; Powell, 1999).

This is done in order to address the questions: By whom is the literacy curriculum defined and how it is implemented? The first step in beginning to answer these questions is to examine the literature that illustrates the ideologies of literacy and the relationship among ideology and the policies that determine both public policy for literacy and bilingual education. In this section, Chapter 1 defines the four common ideologies of schooled literacy, which include functional, cultural, progressive, and critical literacies. Chapter 2 demonstrates how policies for literacy and bilingualism are positioned within very particular ideological orientations. This section concludes with Chapter 3, which considers how our own history and lived experience informs our beliefs and practices, and then examines the hegemony present in literacy curricula and teacher practice.

Chapter 1
Schooled Literacy Ideologies

Education is deeply implicated in the politics of culture. The curriculum is never simply a neutral assemblage of knowledge, somehow appearing in the texts and classrooms of a nation. It is always part of a selective tradition, someone's selection, some group's vision of legitimate knowledge. It is produced out of the cultural, political, and economic tensions and compromises that organize and disorganize a people. (Apple, 1996, p. 22).

Literacy is constructed socially as part of the process of becoming literate and, as such, individuals acquire the norms governing literate behavior within specific social contexts (Powell, 1999). Thus, as stated in the Introduction, the ways in which written language is taught always reflect a particular ideology about what constitutes appropriate literate behavior. However, when literacy instruction, methods, and texts are focused only on pedagogical and procedural issues, the political nature of literacy is never fully revealed. Therefore, any one definition of literacy is at the same time insufficient and complex. Definitions of literacy are always informed and defined within particular historical contexts which are further influenced, and determined, by social factors that change over time and with great variation form one discourse community to another (Williams & Capizzi-Snipper, 1990). Further, "practices of literacy instruction are based upon assumptions about the characteristics and development of literate competence, and they correlatively prescribe functions and uses of literacy in a given society" (Luke, 1988, p. 17).

In order to work toward an understanding of literacy, this chapter will describe the four common *ideologies of literacy* that inform curriculum and pedagogy: functional literacy, cultural literacy, progressive literacy, and critical literacy. Because these are definitions of literacy, it is important to note that all of these forms are understood in contexts where oral language, reading, and writing occur and address questions that go beyond skill level to aim, purpose, audience, and text. In this text I consider them to represent various forms of *schooled ideologies* because each literacy, both oral and written, is "a discourse that carries with it certain expectations for thinking, behaving, and using language" (Powell, 1999, p. 24).

Since the 1800s each ideology of literacy has both influenced the English curricula and has been the fuel for educational and political debates regarding definitions of what it means to be a literate person in school and society. This notion is particularly important when considering ELLs, as these ideologies of schooled literacy are "generally acquired outside one's primary social network" and are "used for gauging success or failure within the institution" (Powell, 1999, p. 24). So, within any approach to literacy there is "an assumption of normative practice, that is, what counts as literacy pedagogically, socially and politically" (Cadiero-Kaplan, 2002, p. 373). It then becomes important to recognize that when addressing school curriculum and methods of teaching literacy, any approach or way of defining what it means to be literate is based on an ideological construct, and as such has the possibility of positioning literacy for either individual empowerment and personal voice, through uses of creative writing, literature, poetry, and narrative critique, or for rudimentary functional job skills, through skills-based curriculum and job preparation writing, which are designed to serve the interests of maintaining the industrial social order (Luke, 1988).

It is such practices and their clear articulation within literacy instruction that is of concern in defining functional, cultural, progressive, and critical ideologies of schooled literacy from a critical pedagogical perspective. It is ideology that first, has the most profound impact on the resulting policy and curricula decisions made from federal to state and local levels of schooling, and is also the least examined in schools of teacher education (Macedo, Dendrinos, & Gounari, 2003).

Functional Literacy

A *functional literacy* ideology is reflected in a curriculum that teaches students the skills deemed necessary to participate in school and society successfully. Most specifically, to have the skills to be a productive citizen and/or member of the work force, and as such, support marketplace ideologies (Apple, 1996; Kelly, 1997). A person who is functionally literate is generally considered an individual who has the ability to read and write in order to complete job applications and other common forms, read and write checks, make shopping lists, and read signs. Most often this is considered to be a fourth to sixth grade level of competency (Williams & Capizzi-Snipper, 1990).

The functionally literate curriculum was originally defined under the premise of *English for All* and focused on "sequential reading skills, grammar skills, and some of the 'basic' cultural information usually found in literature with an emphasis on decoding and analyzing parts of texts-as-objects" (Myers, 1996, p. 34). The materials utilized for teaching basic reading skills are basal readers or graded reading texts; series such as *Open Court* used in many schools would fit this category. Also, word lists such as the Dolch pre-primer word list that was used to assess reading readiness where the curriculum was really

> one part of a 'system for teaching reading'. This system includes the basic books themselves, the workbooks that go with them and the teachers manual which tells what to do with the textbooks, what to do with the workbooks and also tells all of the other activities a teacher should go through in order to do a complete job in teaching reading (Dolch, 1950, p. 319).

The premise of such instruction is that through the use of basal readers and accompanying skill books and drill worksheets, students have the opportunity to learn and practice the skills necessary to comprehend text, with the ultimate goal toward learning to read as opposed to reading to learn. (Shannon, 1989; Myers, 1996).

In this practice, reading is focused on decoding words and analyzing text by answering specific reading comprehension questions both orally and in writing. Comprehension of text is focused on being able to understand vocabulary, directions, and the ability to derive meaning. As such, the functional literature curricula and related instructional practices are "pre-packaged and restrictive; with a pedagogical focus that is individualistic, behaviorist, and competitive" (Kelly, 1997, p. 10). Such instruction does not encourage students to challenge the texts or ideas presented and has the potential to reduce literacy "to the pragmatic requirements of capital; consequently, the notions of critical thinking, culture, and power disappear under the imperatives of the labor process and the need for capital accumulation" (Giroux, 1983, pp. 215–216).

Functional literacy ideology, although presently part of most urban school curricula, historically was most prevalent during the Industrial Revolution and is equated with the school-as-factory model. This form of literacy instruction continues to be part of most curricula and has recently gained conservative support in the development of state standardized testing and the back-to-basics movement and push for state and federal standardized testing and accountability measures. The functional curriculum was traditionally found (and still is) in many skills-based language arts classrooms or remedial English classes. Programs that are skill-based are found in many school districts presently; examples of this curricula include, the Science Research Associates (SRA)/ McGraw-Hill reading series *Open Court* and *Corrective Reading* programs. Both of these widely used reading programs are skill-based curriculum that include graded readers and teacher scripts with segmented level tests. In these programs, teachers put faith in the scientific method of scripted instruction and student compliance and response. Such processes, while effective in increasing phonemic awareness, decoding, and specific comprehension skills are mostly decontextualized, require one specific answer or response, and do not consider the language and/or culture of the students. Further, such functional literacy curricula reinforce job-related skills and behaviors by praising compliance with classroom rules and procedures (Giroux, 1983; Oakes, 1985; Apple, 1986).

One noticeable and disturbing distinction in such skills-based classrooms is that student representation tends to fall along ethnic and class lines, in that the majority of students found in functional literacy classrooms tend to be ethnic minorities and/or are from poor or working-class neighborhoods. Thus, the basic skills curricula becomes the most used and as a result the most valued in creating objectives and outcomes for non-native English speakers and students from poor communities. The devastating result is that "nonstandard literacies of minority groups and the poor are regarded as deficits or deprivations rather than differences" (McLaren, 1988, p. 214). The implications of this ideological approach to programming and instruction in secondary schools is illustrated further in Chapter 5, "Institutional Practices and Effects of Literacy Ideologies."

Cultural Literacy

A *cultural literacy* ideology focuses on the teaching of core cultural beliefs, morality, and common values, with a curriculum that includes the classics or Great Books. In contrast to a functional ideology, a cultural ideology places priority on the information readers bring to discourse and text. That is, in order to comprehend not only written but oral discourse, members of a society or children in a classroom need to have a common background knowledge in order to comprehend the messages received through conversation, newspapers, and other media that report on historical events or engage ideas from world literature and history. As such there is specific cultural knowledge that "all Americans need to know" in order to be successful and competent citizens of society and the world. This literacy specifically consists of a network of information that all competent readers should possess (Hirsch, 1988). Individuals who support and promote a cultural literacy ideology including Allen Bloom, E. D. Hirsch, and William Bennett, assume that this knowledge is common, part of the upper middle-class culture. So, in order for those from lower socioeconomic classes and/or ethnically diverse groups to be successful in school and to have access to mainstream culture, they must be taught this cultural knowledge. I believe that what these authors consider cultural knowledge is actually what critical theorists term cultural capital. "Cultural capital refers to Pierre Bourdieu's concept that different forms of cultural knowledge, such as language, modes of social interaction, and meaning, are valued hierarchically in society" (Leistyna, Woodrum, & Sherblom, 1996, p. 334).

In his introduction to *Cultural Literacy: What Every American Needs to Know*, E. D. Hirsh states that "cultural literacy constitutes the only sure avenue of opportunity for disadvantaged children, the only reliable way of combating the social determinism that now condemns them to remain in the same social and educational condition as their parents" (Hirsch, 1988, p. xiv). It becomes understood then, that by gaining this cultural knowledge students from marginalized communities, including those who speak a language other than English, will be able to more successfully participate in oral and written discourses of the mainstream culture. While this concept may seem altruistic, providing all with a common ground for communication, it is problematic as it negates individual and community experiences. This common knowledge is not only defined by a select group of individuals, but becomes a network of knowledge that consists of "a descriptive list of the information actually possessed by literate Americans" (Hirsch, 1988, p. xiv). Thus the cultural literacy curriculum asserts that through overt instruction and rote memorization of historic facts, literacy passages, and important people one can become culturally literate. However, such a cultural model is derived from overt choices of what to include and exclude from the curriculum, with an assumption that the "whole network of cultural models for any one culture" can be taught, and moreover learned, is very unlikely (Gee, 1990, p. 90).

However, it is just such a process that the ideology of cultural literacy advocates. To be culturally literate, students are taught common core values, morals, and culture, specifically the dominant culture through mainstream history and the Great Books. Presently, such texts as *What Your 4th Grader Needs to Know: Fundamentals of a Good Fourth-Grade Education*, are designed to guide students toward cultural literacy. This type of curriculum is not just narrow in its focus and elite in its content, but is based on a pedagogy of transmission or banking, where the content is conveyed uncritically and taught to be universally understood and common. The curriculum of cultural literacy

> has been with us since the Enlightenment and has long been invoked as an argument for the reproduction of elites. It is a position that advocates a social system in which a select cadre of intellectuals, economically privileged groups, and their professional servants are the only individuals deemed fit to possess the culture's sacred canon of knowledge, which assures their supremacy (Aronowitz & Giroux, 1991, p. 26).

The curriculum of cultural literacy reflects an ideology based in the Western traditions and as such attempts to control not only the spaces where knowledge is produced, but to make a certain core knowledge legitimate. Such literacies are linked to positions of power. Reading (in this tradition) is a process of understanding that reduces the notion of understanding to "learning content deemed appropriate to the well-educated citizen" (Giroux, 1983, p. 212). Within this conservative perspective, the individual experience, if different from that espoused by the canon, is not valued. Thus, the knowledge that is deemed literate by proponents of cultural literacy is one that

> portrays a nation propelled by a harmony of interests, despite internal and external pushes and pulls, that in the end work out of the good of all. De-emphasized in this harmonious view is labor history, women's history, immigrant history, class discord, challenges to capitalism, political dissent, and the

continuous struggle over the purposes of the nation (Coles, 1998, p. 104).

Traditionally the curriculum of cultural literacy has been part of advanced-placement English classes, college preparatory courses, and in many private elite high schools. Such an elitist curriculum is designed to prepare students for positions of power, and as such rejects individual experience while discrediting or ignoring the influences of popular cultures, ethnically and racially diverse cultures, and cultures grounded in sexual communities (i.e., feminist, gay) all of whom, it could be stated, reject the Christian-Judeo ethics that serve as the cornerstone of appropriate morality in such elite cultures (Aronowitz & Giroux, 1991).

In this practice, the individuals for whom this curriculum is supposedly designed are not the ones receiving it. I contend that it is because those students who lack the cultural knowledge are most often found in the functional literacy classrooms. As such, the ideology of cultural literacy, while advocating for the disenfranchised, is positioned to maintain societal inequity. It deems alternative cultural and linguistic discourse communities within this society as illiterate because literacy is determined solely on the basis of knowing and being able to converse, read, and write about those topics that make one literate (McLaren, 1988). However, this ideology does not dismiss the ideology of functional literacy. On the contrary, those advocating for a cultural literacy recognize that the functional skills of decoding and comprehension are necessary in order for students to be successful in reading and having access to the cultural knowledge. As Hirsch (1988) states, "it [cultural literacy] takes no position about methods of initial reading instruction beyond insisting that content must receive as much emphasis as skill" (p. 1). Therefore cultural literacy does little to engage the ideology that informs functional literacy, rather it indirectly supports this ideology and together these ideologies of literacy serve to maintain the status quo.

Cultural literacy, however, is in contrast to progressive literacy, where value is placed on individual experience as a mode of acquisition of skills and knowledge.

Progressive Literacy

In contrast to functional and cultural literacies, *progressive literacy* encourages the inclusion of student voice, culture, and includes a variety of literature and discourses as part of the curriculum. A progressive literacy ideology advocates and encourages personal discovery as a pathway to increasing knowledge. Historically, the goal of teachers of progressive literacy during the 19th century was to "integrate literacy instruction into the curricula based on children's interests, needs, and inclinations; that is, to make literacy a natural consequence of children's study of their physical and social environment" (Shannon, 1989, p. 10). This curriculum is based on many of the democratic ideas postulated by John Dewey (1916) that include the free interchange of ideas between students and educators and the notion of a student-centered curriculum. Such a curriculum attempts to "affirm and legitimize the cultural universe, knowledge, and language practices that students bring into the classroom" (McLaren, 1988, p. 215). A progressive literacy ideology requires students and teachers to engage in the process of learning to read and write based on themes and topics of interest to students, with vocabulary related to the lives of students. This ideology is seen in the whole-language curriculum which is derived from constructivist and cognitive views of learning and is reflected in the use of writer's workshops, literature response journals, and literature circles.

Constructivism is a process that promotes learners as seekers and constructors of knowledge, not receptacles of knowledge. It encourages curiosity and questioning from the student perspective. Thus, social discourse is part of learning, and most importantly, it views students as agents over their learning. Such cognitive processes are supported by Piaget's theory of learning development, which views learning as an active process in which the learner continually constructs meaning. Under the Piagetian model, young children learn to organize their experiences and adapt to their environments through a series of cognitive processes that allow individuals to take in new knowledge in the context of previous experience (Piaget, 1973). This is based on the belief that the construction of meaning and/or knowledge is a dialectical process between readers, text, and the world (Macedo, 1991). Unlike cultural or functional ideologies that define set skills or knowledge bases to access literacy, a progressive approach values the literacy or knowledge discourse the individual brings to the text.

This approach views reading as an intellectual process, "where the comprehension of text is deferred to the development of new cognitive structures which can enable students to move from simple to highly complex reading tasks" (Macedo, 1991, p. 152). This is not to say the mastery of technical skills of decoding and comprehension are not important. Rather, skills are developed with the "explicit recognition of the importance of some form of shared cultural knowledge" (McLaren, 1988, p. 214). Where the functional approach supports teaching the parts that make up the whole, a whole-language theory "exemplifies a constructionist view of learning, according to which concepts and complex processes are constructions of the human brain; therefore, research suggests, the greater the intellectual and emotional involvement in learning, the more effectively the brain learns, uses, and retains what is learned" (Weaver, 1998, p. 7).

Accordingly, a progressive ideology supports whole-language processes because the basic principles of a whole-language approach include the belief that literacy is best developed when individuals make many of their "own decisions about what to read, write, and learn" and, further, will "learn to read and write by being supported in actually reading and writing whole texts—not by being required to do limited activities with bits and pieces of language" (Weaver, 1998, p. 7). In contrast to functional literacy, which reduces reading to a technique of learning to read, progressive forms of literacy support a process of reading to learn. Thus literacy, reading, writing, listening speaking, and thinking develop in an integrated manner where all processes are engaged as part of literacy development. McLaren (1988) cites a passage from Shirley Brice Heath that articulates the importance of reading to learn. She states:

> Readers make meaning by linking the symbols on the page with real-world knowledge and then considering what the text means for generating new ideas and actions not explicitly written or said in the text. The transformation of literacy skills into literate behaviors and ways of thinking depends on a community of talkers who make the text mean something. For most of history, such literate communities have been elite groups, holding themselves and their knowledge and power apart from the masses (from McLaren, 1988, p. 215).

While a progressive ideology values the learner as a knowing subject and provides a space for the individual to construct meaning, it fails, as the other ideologies have, to examine questions of culture, power, and politics. Such practices, while designed to be empowering, are not transformative as they ignore students' cultural capital, which includes their individual lived experiences, histories, languages, and discourse communities. As a result, "students are rarely able to engage in thorough critical reflection, regarding their own practical experience and the ends that motivate them in order, in the end, to organize the findings and thus replace mere opinion about facts with an increasingly rigorous understanding of their significance" (Freire & Macedo, 1987, p. 148).

A progressive ideology appears to be politically neutral and thus does not question the curriculum or engage the sociopolitical context of the curriculum and literacies of students. Additionally, "because literacy is socially constructed, it is erroneous to conceive of literacy as a single, unified entity; rather, we must begin to recognize that there are many different literacies, depending upon the context within which it is to be construed" (Powell, 1999, p. 25). So in order for literacy to become meaningful and historically fluid, a theory of questioning and teaching processes is required that includes critical questions related to how knowledge is produced where teachers and students examine how knowledge is constructed or produced, reproduced or transformed (Macedo, 1991; Macedo et al., 2003). A progressive ideology, however, while valuing the knowledge of the individual, still postulates a curriculum and teaching processes that remains apolitical and unexamined from a critical perspective (Apple, 1986; Freire & Macedo, 1987; McLaren, 1998). This concern is addressed by the fourth ideology, critical literacy.

Critical Literacy

The ideology of *critical literacy* is one "of social transformation in which the ideological foundations of knowledge, culture, schooling, and identity-making are recognized as unavoidably political, marked by vested interests and hidden agendas" (Kelly, 1997, p. 10). This literacy, although student-centered, expands on the progressive notion of personal discovery in that it places both the teacher and student in a historical context and requires both to interrogate the curriculum, which in this literacy, is that of the everyday world. Students involved in a critical literacy curriculum read the world and the word by deconstructing texts and discourses both inside and outside the classroom (Apple, 1986; Kelly, 1997; Powell, 1999).

To better understand critical literacy in relation to other literacies it helps to apply it to the traditions of cultural literacy articulated above and remind educators that "the democratic use of literary canons must always remain critical ... and must justify themselves as representing the elements of our own heritage" (Aronowitz & Giroux, 1991, p. 38). So, rather than reject these cultural texts or functional curricula, a critical literacy approach engages them. This is done by questioning and analyzing the content in relation to the sociopolitical and sociocultural realities of those who read the texts and are supposed to benefit from them. It is within this critical approach that literacy curricula are the most powerful and transforming because such practices take on the texts and discourses of cultural literacy by placing them within a historical and cultural context, providing a sense of place through historicity. Within a critical environment, historicity allows students to read any text or discourse from the perspective of their lives in relation to their present experience (McLaren, 1988; Darder, 1991). Thus, a critical literacy curriculum includes historicity as a core element in reading cultural literacy. This approach requires that students (and teachers) not read history as an unfolding of the Absolute American Spirit and record, that is the truth of American culture and history as commonly told. Rather we are to consider history not as a narrative told from one perspective, but as a record to be held up for examination from other sociocultural and political perspectives (Aronowitz & Giroux, 1991; Macedo, 1994). The concept of historicity of knowledge will be further defined and examined in Chapter 3.

A critical literacy ideology encourages students (and teachers) to deconstruct the myths of civilization and, as such, the cultural literacy canon is "appropriated rather than revered and, with this appropriation, transformed" (Aronowitz & Giroux, 1991, p. 38). However, such transformation is not always desirable within public schools; this sort of critical analysis causes individuals to question what is purported to be "legitimate knowledge" and has the potential to lead students and teachers to deconstruct and unveil hegemonic structures (Aronowitz & Giroux, 1991; Apple, 1995; Macedo, 2003). These critical processes when implemented can pose a threat to the dominant school culture, most often reflected in functional and cultural literacies, which function to "legitimate the interests and values of dominant groups while it marginalizes and disconfirms essential knowledge and experiences of subordinate and oppressed groups" (Aronowitz & Giroux, 1985, p. 147). Therefore, a critical literacy approach has the potential to promote critical thinking and further transform curriculum and instruction to meet the interests of minority groups, which in many urban schools across our country actually reflect the majority of a school culture.

If this is the case, then a new definition of literacy is needed one that acknowledges the hegemonic power structure and values the discourses of groups that have traditionally been marginalized in schools and society:

> such a literacy would enable students to question and to engage in critical dialogue so that they might be educated for participation in a democracy. It would provide a means for identifying and reflecting upon those ideological and social conditions that serve to profit a few at the expense of many (Powell, 1999, p. 20).

As with cultural ideology, the critical theorist does not reject the need for students to have the functional skills necessary to read and write. That is, as within both cultural and progressive literacies, in order to be critically literate, individuals also need to know how to decode text and comprehend it so they can then engage critically the messages the text carries. However, adherents of progressive or critical literacy processes must be cautious not to create situations

> in which students ultimately find themselves held accountable for knowing a set of rules (functional) about which no one has ever directly informed them. Teachers do students no service to suggest, even implicitly, that "product" is not important. In this country, students will be judged on their product regardless of the process they utilized to achieve it. And that product, based as it is on the specific codes of a particular culture, is more readily produced when the directives of how to produce are made explicit (Delpit, 1995, p. 31).

This positions literacy beyond the mere skills of orality, reading, and writing, but rather takes up literacy as social action. I therefore advocate here a multiple-process approach to literacy. Critics of this text could argue that progressive and critical approaches to literacy development are not forms of schooled literacy ideologies, because they are designed to engage the individual in evaluating and deconstructing school texts found in both functional and cultural literacy perspectives. I contend that in order for students to have access to any one particular ideology or form, it is within the context of schools that such critique and engagement occur. In this sense I view any literacy ideology as a schooled concept. Thus, while I support more critical and progressive ideologies of literacy, those of functional and cultural literacy cannot be dismissed, as they have the potential to inform engagement in text and provide the space and potential to "re-define 'cultural' literacy to include the culture of the many as opposed to the few" (Cadiero-Kaplan, 2002, p. 380).

As teachers and educators, we do not typically view *literacy as both pedagogy and social action*. Traditionally, literacy is viewed as a method that is scientific, apolitical, and ahistorical. Based on this review it is "evident that schools have not traditionally been encouraged to teach all discourses; rather they have been commissioned to teach a particular discourse, or form of literacy—a literacy that is sanctioned by dominant groups" (Powell, 1999, p. 13) or scientific methods supported by specific political agendas (Taylor, 1998). Thus, schools have not readily accepted the teaching of critical literacy, for it reveals the underlying hegemony in literacy practices and, further, within school practices and curriculum. Giroux (1987) states that

> Gramsci viewed literacy as both a concept and a social practice that must be linked historically to configurations of knowledge and power, on the one hand, and the political and cultural struggle over language and experience on the other. For Gramsci, literacy was a double-edged sword; it could be wielded for the purpose of self and social empowerment or for the perpetration of relations of repression and domination (pp. 1–2).

Thus, literacy curricula decisions are most often the result of conscious choices that are inextricably tied to the political and economic structures of our country. Further, these decisions are inherently ideological in that they are "qualified by the context of assumptions, beliefs, values, expectations, and related conceptual material that accompany their use by particular groups of people in particular socio-historical circumstances" (Knoblauch & Brannon, 1993, p. 15). So the manner in which literacy, and further language, is taught is based within a particular ideology that clearly defines literate acts through reading, writing, and engagement with text (Powell, 1999). Therefore, teachers and educators must be cautious not to confuse "*what is* with *what must be*" and not fail to recognize that "common practices come not from divining decree, but from choices made sometime, somewhere" (Hinchey, 1998, p. 7) by individuals within specific historical and cultural contexts that further support the greater political and economic structures of our society.

This analysis of ideology alone is insufficient to thoroughly comprehend how ideology and politics translates into school policy and further to teacher practice. The next step is to engage these ideologies with forms of literacy (i.e., oral, written, spoken, etc.) that connect with public policy for English and bilingual instruction in schools. In the following chapter, a Framework for Engaging Literacy Ideology Policy

& Practice will be presented that illustrates historically how functional, cultural, progressive, and critical ideologies inform particular forms and public policies for both literacy and bilingual education. Part II of this text takes this analysis even further, to teaching approaches and curriculum for language development.

Reflective Activity: Take a moment to respond to the following questions. After writing, discuss your response with one or two other people.

1) What is your understanding of ideology?

2) What does it mean to be literate in our society?

3) Define the following: school literacy, home literacy, community literacy, personal literacy.

4) How does each ideology of literacy inform or relate to your responses above?

5) What aspects of each ideology do you agree with? Disagree with? Why?

Chapter 2
Public Policy:
Literacy & Bilingual Education

Teaching English ... is based on the universal capability of children and is not based on a universal model of intelligence or a universal model of literacy. English and other school subjects are shaped by a nation's national policy on minimum literacy. Thus our models of mental functioning are, within universal biological constraints, socially constructed and socially contingent upon the specific literacy policies which we use to structure relationships between ourselves and our environment, between our voice and other voices within our own heads, all for the purpose of exploring, expressing, and shaping inner and outer worlds (Myers, 1996, pp. 2–3).

There has been little attempt in the past or present to articulate the connections among literacy policy, bilingual education policies, and ideology of literacy. In my review of public policy literacy and bilingual education I sought to draw the articulation of these educational policies together by drawing from two core sources in the field of literacy / reading education and bilingual education. Miles Myers and his text *Changing Our Minds: Negotiating English and Literacy* set out to define the United States policies for literacy instruction from the 1600s to the present and connect them to ideology and teacher practice. Colin Baker has authored a key text, *Foundations of Bilingual Education and Bilingualism*, where he reviews the program models and history of bilingual education policy as it has emerged in this country. I want to acknowledge the work of these authors as their writings have contributed in part to the formulation of this policy review.

In this text I have taken their historical reviews and definitions of these literacy and program policies to inform and reveal the sociopolitical connections to forms of literacy ideologies and ultimately to teacher practice. This historical analysis is significant because it is from the public policy arena that most decisions regarding curriculum, programming, and pedagogy are made in schools. These critical decisions result in the promotion of one "correct form" of literacy or definition of bilingual programming, which then becomes directly tied to processes for teaching language to both monolingual English and linguistic minority students in our schools. In order to transform schools, I believe it is time for teachers across programs to come together to examine the ideological connections for literacy and biliteracy development. While I don't directly discuss biliteracy models here, I ultimately advocate bi- and multiple- literacy models. In order to achieve a biliteracy model however, it is imperative that all educators, monolingual and bilingual, understand how these two separate policies are actually informed and politicized to divide the education of language minority students from English, rather than focus on processes for quality education models, toward which this analysis is focused.

Myers's (1996) ideas regarding the teaching of English demonstrate how a form of literacy is linked not only to political ideologies, but to legitimate forms of literacy development. Where public policy literacy is defined as "a set of sanctioned communication practices with assigned political authority and social status given to selected sign systems" (Myers, 1996, p. 119). Such literacies are deemed legitimate forms by policy makers, and as such have a direct impact on both literacy and other school curricula and practices in unique ways. As depicted in Table 1, the Framework for Engaging Literacy Ideology Policy & Practice, each of the four ideologies of literacy—functional, cultural, progressive, and critical—presented in the previous chapter, can be contextualized within certain historical time frames and policies of public literacy. The four main public policies, as outlined by Myers (1996), and the time period of their dominance are:

1. Oral to Signature and Recording Literacy, beginning in the 17th and 18th centuries through the early 19th century.
2. Recitation and Report Literacy, from the late 19th to early 20th centuries.
3. Literacy of Decoding, Defining and Analyzing, beginning in the early 1900s (although Myers places this through 1983, I would argue that it is still a form valued by many conservatives who are fostering the efforts toward the "back to basics" movement and era of standardized testing (Hirsch, 1988; Bennett, 1995; Ravitch, 1995; Murnane & Levy, 1996).

4. Transition to a New Standard of Literacy, from the 1960s to the early 1980s.

Table 1: Framework for Engaging Literacy Ideology Policy & Practice

Time Period	Public Policy Literacy	Literacy Ideology	Bilingual Education	Teaching & Program Approaches
1600	Oral	Progressive	Permissive	Communicative Approach
1700	Signature			Whole Language Native Language Instruction
1800				
1860	Recording, Recitation, Report	Functional, Cultural		Phonics & Skills Grammar Method Great Books
1900			Restrictive	
1916	Decoding, Defining, Analyzing	Functional		Decoding, Phonics, Basal Readers, English Submersion
1940				
1950	New Standards	Critical	Opportunity	Whole Language
1970		Progressive		Progressive Literacy Critical Literacy Dual Language &
1983				Maintenance Programs Communicative Approach
1990	Decoding, Defining, Analyzing	Functional Cultural	Dismissive	English Immersion Phonics/Skills Cultural Literacy Standardized Instruction
Present 2000–2004		Functional		

This chapter aligns these four forms of public policy literacy to bilingual education policy within the same time periods and further articulates them within specific ideologies: functional, cultural, progressive, and critical literacy. Before making the connection to bilingual education policy, it is important to first understand two prevailing political views of bilingual education, which have a direct impact on how each is understood. Brisk (1998) defines bilingual education as either "compensatory education" or "quality education" (see Table 2). According to Brisk, a *compensatory education* policy focuses on the choice of language, where the policy makers determine which language of instruction will be utilized. Within this model the overriding goal of education is to "teach students English as quickly as possible." Since "English is viewed as the only means for acquisition of knowledge, students' fluency in English is the essential condition to receiving an education" (Brisk, 1998, p. xviii). This latter view is most prevalent today in many schools.

Table 2: Compensatory Education versus Quality Education

	Compensatory Education	*Quality Education*
Policy	Choice of language instruction	Right to good education
Pedagogy	• Search for the best model to teach English • Education is possible only in English	• Effective schools, advances in education • Language and culture of students are vehicles for education
Expected Outcomes	• English proficiency	• Academic achievement • English proficiency • Varying degrees of native language proficiency • Sociocultural integration

From *Bilingual Education: From Compensatory to Quality Schooling* (p. xix), by M. E. Brisk, 1998, Mahwah, NJ: Lawrence Erlbaum Associates. Copyright 1998 by Lawrence Erlbaum Associates, Inc. Reprinted with permission.

Conversely, a *quality education* policy focuses on a student's right to a good education with the goal being "to educate students to their highest potential" where English is only a part of the educational goal. In a quality model, "bilingual learners access knowledge not only through English but through their native languages" (Brisk, 1998, p. xix); there is a recognition and value for their cultural experiences and knowledge. These altering views of bilingual education are important to keep in mind when considering the literacy and bilingual policy reviewed below. As indicated in Table 1, each view of literacy policy and bilingual education is linked to an ideological construct. The ideological constructs of bilingual education are thus informed by the definitions of educational policy and pedagogy illustrated in Table 2. That is, language policy for bilingual programs can either be one that focuses on choice of language instruction or one that is premised on the right to good education. In the following literature the policy and pedagogy of both compensatory and quality models will be seen in various time periods.

Baker (1996) has identified four overlapping periods of bilingual education policy:

- The Permissive Period: 18th and 19th centuries
- The Restrictive Period: 1900–1940
- Period of Opportunity: 1950s–1970s
- The Dismissive Period: 1980s to present

Baker (1996) points out: "These periods are not neat in their divisions and, in each period, there are variations in different States in policies and practices" (p. 166). However, these periods reflect the general shift in perspectives of politicians, administrators, educators, and in school practice that are indicators of discernible shifts in ideology, pedagogy, and practice. The periods of bilingual policy have been defined here within the context of the eras of public policy literacy.

The framework and this chapter provide a parallel analysis of public policy literacy and bilingual education policy as depicted in Table 1. This analysis is necessary in order to illustrate the connections between politics and educational policy making because within much of the literature and research on bilingual education, "the degree of sentiment evoked by bilingual education is not matched by an equivalent degree of understanding about the history of language minority education in the United States, or by knowledge about the state of bilingual education" (Malakoff and Hakuta, 1990, p. 27) or an adequate knowledge of literacy policy making that results in language arts and English curricula.

In this section I articulate the connection between pedagogy and practice with certain forms of literacy and educational policy. Such a critical evaluation reveals both the ideologies and policies that support or negate effective programming and pedagogy for students at the secondary level. Further, this analysis provides a framework, as illustrated in Table 1, to critically engage past and present bilingual education policy and practice in the context of ideology of literacy and public policy. The historical time periods are meant to be markers to view the historical development over time. They are not meant to be finite periods, but ranges to place literacy, policy, and bilingual education within their corresponding historical, social, and political contexts. The last column of the framework, "Teaching & Programming Approaches," will be addressed directly in Chapter 4.

Literacy and Bilingual Education Policy: 1600 to 1864

Oral Literacy to Signature and Recording Literacy

> *Every teacher who faces a classroom is facing many layers of historical assumptions about how literacy should be defined. Part of the art and science of teaching is learning how to help students get "through" these layers of folklore and history to an understanding of contemporary conceptions of literacy. A teacher, then is not just teaching reading or writing—some absolute mental activity which everyone accepts as the goal of schools. Teachers are teaching contingent definitions and constructions of reading and writing* (Myers, 1996, p. 60).

During the 1600s and early 1700s oral forms of communication were dominant and, at that time, superior to written or printed literature forms. Interestingly, reading oftentimes implied "hearing by attending lectures and listening" (Myers, 1996 p. 30). During this period, an individual's word or statement was taken to be truth, and most people believed that written documents were unreliable. Politically it was believed that print undermined local authority and thus great value was placed on visuals, the spoken word, and an individual's immediate memory. Such practices encouraged a highly decentralized system of governance, with value being placed on community networks and group solidarity (Street, 1984; Myers, 1996). Oral literacy is based on social context and is directed to an individual with the goal of influencing the listener's views, maintaining a certain relationship or controlling an individuals actions. Oral literacy is highly contextual with communication that "can be constantly modified according to its effect and thus the social function dominates the logical" (Street, 1984, p. 20). For small communities this form of literacy is trusted over communication that is decontextualized (i.e., letter writing, government documents) and most often comes from outside the community. Further, "language in an oral culture often does not have 'outside' textual references to which we can turn for an outside definition, and thus, definitions in many 'oral' usages are often inside the local group" (Myers, 1996, p. 26).

In the 1700s we began to see a transition from oral, face-to-face literacy, to print literacy. The transfer to a print literacy began during the colonization of the United States. It was one of the most powerful methods utilized to colonize and control other people and was part of the process of establishing more centralized forms of government (Cohen, 1982). "The Greeks used paper, the Greek alphabet, and writing as 'the first great sledgehammer blows of technology' to replace the clay tablets of oral cultures and to take power way from the decentralized local governments of oral cultures in Greek city-states" (Myers, 1996, pp. 30–31).

It is not surprising that there was much resistance to this transformation into print culture by the Greeks of the ancient past, as well as the Anglo-Saxons of the American colonies. Such points of resistance may also be seen today among students in our classrooms. In many communities, both in school and at home, children may not have access to books or writing materials, but may be told stories, be encouraged to ask questions and relate experiences, or engage in drawing or physical action to communicate messages or comprehension of knowledge. Wells (1981) found that children who came to school with a concept of print literacy (i.e., are read to, practice writing, etc.) are located in a cultural space that views print as the legitimate form of literacy, a view that tends to match the form of literacy valued in our schools. So, from as early as preschool, children who come from an oral literate culture may be seen as underprepared or illiterate by many teachers, reading specialists, and school administrators. When considering Native American languages for example, words are not symbols for meaning— word and meaning are one experience with the spoken word being sacred. Thus, "as an historically oral culture, there is likely to be a very unwieldy fit with the world of artificial school language" and the child's home community (Courts, 1997, p. 15). These concepts are not just historically true, but presently reflected in national policies for literacy and language instruction, where print literacy is viewed as a mechanism of the status quo and necessary to success.

Historically the society of the late 1700s to the mid-1800s moved from a signature to a recording literacy. Travel in the 1700s began the shift in social practices from "face-to-face interactions with acquaintances, to interactions with strangers, and as a result, the literacy standard of the colonies began to shift" (Myers, 1996, p. 32). Signatures and written records became more legitimate than the spoken word. During the latter part of this historical period, newspapers, books, sermons, legal codes, and pamphlets became prevalent and valued; "He who is unable to write his name and make his mark is, not withstanding, a competent and legal witness to the execution of a will" (Stevens cited in Myers, 1996, pp. 44–45). Those individuals regarded in high status were those who could sign their names and both read and write. An "X" mark was considered to be a signature by those who could not write their names, while most literate individuals had unique signatures. Additionally, signatures of the time usually included some artistic embellishment that identified the individual.

Throughout the early days of signature literacy in England and the United States, "the alphabet did not have the same personal significance or moral force as a picture or other visual mark, and as a result, many people placed the cross upon legal documents to invoke religious authority" (Campbell & Quinn and Cressy, cited in Myers, 1996, p. 40). Still others used very personal marks to invoke ownership or family tradition. These practices continue in classrooms today. Some teachers add smiles (ü) and exclamations (!) to their notes, and students practice over and over again the art of their own signature. Many elementary students mix together pictures and the alphabet, and still others draw pictures to tell stories (Myers, 1996, p. 40).

Forms of writing increased from 1776 to 1895 and ranged from those who did not know their letters, to those who could read the Bible, and "in the middle range were those who could write using invented spelling" (Myers, 1996, p. 45). Public documents representative of this middle range were usually handbills, posters, and announcements. In homes, the most common texts were the Bible and the almanac, while in schools the goal was to "teach students how to sign their names, copy words, read essential words, do simple calculations," and "to have some awareness of how devotional books were organized, and to know some religious passages by heart" (Myers, 1996, p. 49). This process from signature to recording literacies reflects a shift in purpose from artistic forms of handwriting to that of contracts and legal documents, to establishing national cohesion among immigrants and new urban populations, reflecting the ideologies of those in power in society at that time.

Bilingual Education: The Permissive Period (18th and 19th Centuries)

Although the hegemony of English over the thirteen colonies had been decided by the late seventeenth century, the sounds of German, Dutch, French, Swedish, Irish, and Welsh were frequently heard at the time of the American Revolution, and Spanish was dominant in several soon-to-be-acquired territories (Crawford, 1999, p. 21).

During the 18th and early 19th centuries, linguistic diversity was generally accepted and often encouraged (Brice-Heath, 1976; Baker, 1996; Crawford, 1999). The use of languages other than English was accepted as the norm and encouraged through religion and with the printing of newspapers in different languages. In the 18th century, "newspaper advertisements for runaway servants, both black and white, made frequent reference to their bilingual or trilingual proficiencies" (Crawford, 1999, p. 21), as depicted in the following ad that appeared in 1776:

June 8, 1776 Runaway Servant: Virginia Gazette

FIVE POUND REWARD. RUN away from the Subscriber, in Suffolk, in the Night of Wednesday the 4th Instant [June] a Dutch Servant Man named JOHN CHARLES KITTLER, who is Breeches-Maker by Trade, but may pass for a Tailor, he is about 5 Feet 6 or 7 inches high, and about 23 Year of age, slender made, of a fair complexion, and had long yellow hair; Language: speaks good French, and several other languages, but bad English language.

In Philadelphia during the late 17th century, both private and public schools in German were common, with some being bilingual and others being German only (Baker, 1996; Crawford, 1999). Such support of linguistic diversity was supported by the Continental Congress, which "agreed that any and all languages could be used as instruments for spreading communication necessary to legitimate the political system within the new nation." Initially "the use of languages other than English was encouraged and looked upon by national leaders with favor, because of both practical advantages and opportunities for the expansion of knowledge different languages offered" (Brice-Heath, 1976, pp. 12–13). However, the reason for political support of bilingual schools and a linguistically diverse society was not supported solely for intellectual development, but more as a political need to assist in uniting a nation (Brice-Heath, 1976; Brisk, 1998). This impetus for societal cohesion through the support of native-language use and schooling is also seen in California of the 1700s, where the mission system was entrenched and

> it became standard policy within each of the missions to teach the young Indian boys Spanish so that they could become proficient interpreters for the padres. At most missions, mass and daily affairs were conducted in two languages (Estrada, 1979, p. 100).

During this period, on the west coast of the United States, many priests and Indians were bilingual or trilingual, with Spanish being the dominant language (Estrada, 1979; Brisk, 1998).

These trends of openness in foreign language instruction were also reflected in the movement of literacy from signature to recording, where the need or purpose of literacy was becoming that of contracts and legal documents. Advanced processes were deemed necessary in establishing cohesion among immigrant groups and urban populations across the country. This movement is further reflected in the number of non-English dominant public and private schools that existed between 1839 and 1880. During this period there were German schools in the Midwest, French schools in Louisiana, and Spanish schools in New Mexico (Alexander & Nava, 1976; Crawford, 1999).

"This openness to in-migrant languages in the latter of half of the 19th century was partly motivated by competition for students between public and private schools" (Baker, 1996, p. 166). In practical reality, however, the permissive public policy regarding the learning of other languages was for political and economic national security, not for individual empowerment. Brice-Heath (1976) notes two important factors supporting this assertion:

> German and French armed forces played important roles during the Revolution; many of those who remained after the War became economically, politically, and socially prominent, while retaining their native tongues. The founding fathers often pointed out the advantages of multilingualism for both individual benefits and national service. Thomas Jefferson advised his daughter

and young correspondents to learn French and Spanish—French not only for
its obvious importance in diplomatic affairs, but also for the access it provided
to publications presenting recent advancements in science (pp. 12–13).

Students attending English schools that taught German, French, or Spanish were not representative of the masses. On the contrary, schooling
during this period was mostly for those in power positions or the elite
classes of the time (Crawford, 1999).

Again, this trend is also seen on the west coast, through the mission
system, which served the dominant power structure of Europeans from
Spain. For example, it was the policy of the Spanish government to
keep the *indio in pueblos* or at the mission in separate *rancherias* … with
the Indian women living in *monjerias* training in domestic services "while
the young children received training in reading, writing, and technical
trades" (Estrada, 1979, p. 99). Thus, the purpose of bilingual schooling
in California in the late 18th and early 19th centuries was to assimilate
the indigenous population with the emphasis on maintaining the mission facilities and "to engender citizenship and community life"
(Estrada, 1979, p. 99). In distinct contrast to the present, leaders of that
century valued political liberty over linguistic homogeneity (Crawford,
1999), which resulted in no uniform policy regarding language of school
instruction during the 1700s and early 1800s; as a consequence

> more than a dozen states passed laws that provided for schooling in languages
> other than English, either as subject or as a medium of instruction. Even with-
> out explicit legal authorization, local school boards provided classes in lan-
> guages as diverse as Swedish, Danish, Norwegian, Italian, Polish, Dutch, and
> Czech (Crawford, 1999, pp. 23–24).

Actually, it wasn't until the beginning of the Common School Movement, which coincided with an influx of new immigrant groups to the
United States, that policies toward language instruction became more
implicated in the teaching learning process.

Literacy and Bilingual Education Policy: 1864 to 1917

Recitation and Report Literacy

> *Now, as in much of the nineteenth century, literacy achievement is determined as
> much or more by the needs of those who control society's political economy than by the
> instructional approaches teachers choose* (Coles, 1998, p. 137).

It was during this period of time that the emphasis on morals education was introduced in the schools literacy curriculum. This was also the time of the Common School Movement, where states offered compulsory public education (Myers, 1996; Coles, 1998). The focus of instruction was on morals and cultural literacy. The teaching approaches of this time were based on the ideas postulated by Johan Herbart of Germany, who believed that "morality was both the foundation and the goal of education" where morality education focused on five core teaching principles: "inner freedom, perfection, benevolence or good will, justice, and equity or retribution" (Rippa, 1988, p. 169). The teaching of these ideas was mediated through student memorization and recitations of a variety of texts by prominent writers of the time, such as Hugh Blair and John Bartlett, whose texts could be contextualized as a catechism of cultural information. This approach to literacy can be seen as a forerunner to E. D. Hirsch, editor of the series of texts beginning with *Cultural Literacy: What Every American Needs to Know*. The purpose of this book series is to provide readers with factual historical information, with topics ranging from the birth of the silicon chip to the date and location of the Civil War (Hirsch, 1988). This listing of facts is taken up in much the same way that Blair and Bartlett's work was in the late 19th century, where intelligence was equated with how much written materials a student could memorize and recite (Myers, 1996). In grade schools, texts such as Noah Webster's "The American Spelling Book," John and Jane (pre-Dick & Jane), and other basal series increased in popularity and were the core materials utilized to teach reading (Shannon, 1989).

Interestingly, most of the reading during this historical period was intended to reflect real life; however, the lifestyles depicted in the majority of texts represented mostly white, middle-class values and ideals. Literacy at this time reflected knowledge of the cultural canon and the ability to read a variety of texts deemed valuable by the political structure. It is important to note that the common schools began by providing education not for the benefit of all children, but for the children of the wealthy. Many children did not attend school but instead needed to work in order to help support their families, enabling those with political-economic power to benefit from child labor, resulting in minimal literacy of these child workers (Rippa, 1988; Coles, 1998). Meanwhile, critique and questioning of the content and the texts utilized were not part of the teaching/learning process; those who questioned the content or processes or didn't toe the line, usually left school (Rippa,

1988; Coles, 1998). The growth of the common schools during this period came out of demands of many labor leaders who were concerned with the increase of child labor and poor working conditions (Rippa, 1988).

Presently we are in a political state where much of this rhetoric is being reasserted in the "back to basics" movement, the need for morals education (Bennett, 1995), and federal polices such as No Child Left Behind that dictate core-curriculum and testing outcomes based on discrete knowledge components. Although many books are published today that reflect our society's ethnic and cultural diversity, on the whole, the "majority continue to depict, as school reading primers always have, a moral imperative that reinforces the organization of the societal order" (Coles, 1998, p. 95). Interestingly, previous to this century "recitation was the last literacy period in the U.S. when teachers entered classrooms with unquestioned authority over knowledge" (Myers, 1996, p. 80). Such an environment was possible because the teacher and the texts were "the one source of knowledge and moral authority" (Myers, 1996, p. 80). Further, this method of orality is a stark contradiction to oral literacy, in that the oral is derived from written text rather than from face-to-face interactions that are the basis of primary orality. In our media-laden society of the 21st century, such "secondary orality has become one of the [most] dominant forms of communication" (Myers, 1996, p. 78).

The prevalent cultural-ideological direction at that time was the melting pot, and the government, in response to the Civil War, felt a need to establish and create a cohesive social order; one which would reflect the values and norms of the ruling white, Protestant, middle class. Those with the means felt the need and duty to control the masses. Such acts, then as now, only serve to bolster the powers of those individuals whose ethnicity and values are reflective of the dominant political-economic structure, while lowering and deeming inappropriate those who are not (Giroux, 1983; Shannon, 1989; Macedo, 1994).

Then as now, however, there were many advocates for a more humanizing and child-centered pedagogy. In 1875, Francis Parker of Quincy, Massachusetts, promoted one of several countermethods that began to emerge. Parker advocated a form of literacy instruction that went beyond memorization and recitation. He believed that the curriculum needed to include children's lives and interests as a core goal.

Parker, who had studied the work of Pestalozzi, Froebel, and Herbar in Europe, advocated a literacy curriculum based on the idea that students learn to read as they learn to talk; that is, by discussing topics of interest, writing about them and then reading their own words in a supportive atmosphere. Parker believed that spelling could best be learned through authentic writing exercises, with students using their own vocabulary (Shannon, 1989). The local school board challenged this practice because it did not support the model of the teacher as transmitter and holder of knowledge, and further did not support the market economy that placed value on a more scientific approach to reading and literacy. The ideology of Parker and others of this time is reflective of a progressive literacy that advocates a more student-centered approach, and can be seen in the whole-language practices of today. The tension that began at the beginning of the 20th century between the scientific approach to literacy development and more progressive student-centered practices was the beginning of what has now become known as the *phonics versus whole language debate* (Shannon, 1989; Myers, 1996; Coles, 1998).

The teaching of morals and the cultural canon, as policy for common schools, had the most support as policy after the Civil War when the number of immigrants coming to United States increased (Baker, 1996; Myers, 1996). It is important to note that prior to the Civil War, most non-English-speaking immigrants to the eastern shores of the United States were from Germany; however, during the post–Civil War period, the majority of immigrants came from the non-English-speaking nations of Russia, Austria, Hungary, and Italy in the eastern and middle regions of the United States (Leibowitz, 1984). At the same time, the population in the states of California, Arizona, New Mexico, Texas, and Colorado were mostly Spanish speaking (Estrada, 1979). Immigration patterns began to increase significantly after the beginning of the Civil War, "from 1815–1860, five million people came; from 1860 to 1890, 10 million; and from 1890 to 1914, 15 million" (Liebowitz, 1984, p. 30). This increase in a more diverse population impacted not only the policy for literacy instruction, but brought to the forefront issues regarding the use of languages other than English and bilingual education.

Bilingual Education: The Restrictive Period

One of the most fascinating aspects of bilingualism in the United States is the extreme instability, for it is a transitional stage toward monolingualism in English. Each new wave of immigrants has brought with it its own language and then witnessed the erosion of that language in the face of the implicitly acknowledged public language, English (Hakuta, 1986, p. 166).

Due to the increase in immigration toward the end of the 19th century and early part of the 20th century, there was a great concern about or fear of foreigners by the majority English-speaking population. In response to this fear there was a call for Americanization, with an emphasis on integration, harmonization, and assimilation of immigrants (Baker, 1996; Crawford, 1999). What emerged was "the image of the immigrant as unlettered and easily corrupted," which "focused attention on education and the English language as the unifying and uplifting element." In writing about public sentiment toward immigration policy during the late 1800s, Dorman B. Easton, author of the 1898 publication, the *Civil Service Reformer*, stated his abhorrence to newcomers, saying they were "humiliating to an American patriot" (Leibowitz, 1984, p. 31).

Thus, the "immigrants' lack of English language and literacy was seen as a source of social, political, and economic concern" (Baker, 1996, p. 167). As a result, competence in English became associated with patriotism and loyalty to the United States. The first political response to such sentiment began with adducing concerns regarding which citizens could be employed by the federal government. In 1882 the Pendleton Act established the Civil Service Merit System. This act limited federal government employment to citizens who were able to complete a required examination given in English; the successful completion of this exam was a prerequisite for obtaining public office (Brice-Heath, 1976; Leibowitz, 1984). As a result, state and local governments passed similar legislation regarding employment within their governmental offices (Baker, 1996; Wiley, 1996).

In regards to becoming a citizen, the Nationality Act of 1906 required immigrants to speak English prior to becoming naturalized Americans (Leibowitz, 1984). Accordingly, the policy for education and socialization of immigrants became more important than filling the work force; that is, it was more important to advocate for child "literacy in English rather than child labor" and to have immigrants "socialized into a unified America rather than have ethnic separation with increased centralized control." Such sentiment "led to a belief in a common language for compulsory schooling" (Baker, 1996, p. 167).

These views of immigrants were also reflected in the educational policy taking place in California, for as early as 1855 and reemerging today, the state legislature passed a law that all instruction in public schools be conducted in English (Brisk, 1998). "This action, intended apparently to guarantee 'Americanization' of all children, instead excluded most Spanish-speaking children from public education and had the unintended result of spurring the creation of parochial schools in the state" (Estrada, 1979, p. 102). Within these schools, pupils were taught in both Spanish and English. This practice coincided with the response in the Midwest and east where private schools taught immigrants in German, French, and Dutch, along with English. The major factor that influenced the repression of linguistic diversity during this era was the involvement of the United States in the First World War, which began in 1917, when

> linguistic diversity was replaced by linguistic intolerance. School became the tool for assimilation and integration of diverse languages and cultures. Socialization into being American meant the elimination of languages and cultures other than English from schools (Baker, 1996, p. 167).

This is in sharp contrast to years earlier where, in 1910, there were nine million German-Americans living and struggling to maintain their language and culture in the United States. This maintenance was accomplished through religious schools and community groups along with German-language newspapers, and German instruction in both public and private schools (Leibowitz, 1984; Hakuta, 1986; Brisk, 1998).

The attitude of linguistic intolerance in schools, while beginning in the late 19th century, continued well into the 20th century. The impact of such intolerance is reflected in the law for mandatory public school attendance of all children in 1820. To entice students to attend, the public schools began by using the language of the community. As a result, private schools lost not only funding from the states, but attendance. So, as the attendance in public schools increased, the use of community languages in schools decreased (Brice-Heath, 1976); and "by 1923, thirty-four states had decreed that English must be the sole language of instruction in all elementary schools, public and private" (Baker, 1996, p. 167). It's also significant to point out that the immigrant population of the late 19th and early 20th centuries had transformed:

> The older immigrants tended to be urban intellectuals who used prestige languages like French or German. The newer immigrants, on the other hand, were

very often rural peasants who did not command a prestige language. In fact, many of the newer groups had less desire to maintain all of their old ways; they wanted to begin a new life in America, which meant learning English and adopting American values (Stoller, 1977, pp. 48–49).

This combination of a more culturally and linguistically diverse immigrant population, a negative reaction toward linguistic diversity by policy makers, and an increase in urban public schools, had a direct impact on the policies that began to emerge regarding the teaching of literacy for a society moving toward industrialization. The following section examines the beginning and growth of the policy supporting the scientific approach to reading instruction.

Literacy and Bilingual Education Policy: 1916 to 1983

Literacy of Decoding, Defining and Analyzing

Two ideals are struggling for supremacy in American life today: one, the industrial idea, dominating thru the supremacy of commercialism, which subordinates the worker to the product and the machine; the other, the ideal democracy, the ideal of the educators, which places humanity above all machines, and demands that all activity shall be the expression of life (Haley, 1904, quoted in Myers, 1996, p. 85).

The above statement, although written in 1904, could easily have been made today with the most recent attempts to standardize curriculum, place teachers as technicians, and to leave no child behind. The ending time period of this literacy period in some respects is incorrect because the literacy of decoding, defining, and analyzing did not occur in a singular time period. As depicted in Table 1, and reviewed within a functional ideology in the previous chapter, the resulting policy of decoding historically has been grounded as one end of a pendulum's swing with ideological regularity in our country. A functional ideology tends to prevail when the status quo is threatened by diversity and there is a move toward decentralization of educational control (Apple, 1979; Apple, 1995; Coles, 1998; Taylor, 1998; Coles, 2000).

Beginning in 1916, the scientific approach toward reading instruction gained popularity and momentum as a reaction to the recitation method (Myers, 1996). Alongside this movement, in the early part of the 20th century, were educators who advocated that students needed to move away from strict recitation and memorization of great texts, and begin to define and analyze such canonical readings, and demonstrate their comprehension abilities (Luke, 1988; Shannon, 1989; Apple, 1995; Myers, 1996; Coles, 1998). Thus, decoding reflected the scientific approach with defining and analyzing as part of the process. The ultimate goal was for teachers to teach students to read and understand what they had read. During recitation literacy, understanding of the text was not essential to reading it. However, under the scientific paradigm, it was believed that teachers needed clear instructions on how to teach reading, not memorization, and to be able to assess student comprehension of text in order to ensure the ability of individuals to read novel texts and derive meaning (Goodman, 1986; Myers, 1996; Coles, 1998). This approach to reading reflected the growing national interest and obsession in measuring literacy and intelligence. This *testing* period was a reaction to xenophobia with respect to non-English-speaking immigrants, racism toward African Americans and other racial minority groups, and concerns regarding the large number of Army recruits who were failing entrance tests (Wiley, 1996; Myers, 1996). Beginning in 1917, a massive testing campaign was initiated with testing materials developed and paid for by corporate foundations to conduct research in the areas of studies on the inheritance of mental traits, eugenics, and race betterment. This research although acknowledging that

> English literacy and some formal schooling were requisite for intelligence testing, ... [the researchers of] the period paid little heed to language, class, and culture bias and presented their findings as "objective," "empirica'" evidence that those of Anglo-Saxon origin were of "superior" intellectual and moral stock. In the United States, the so-called, "scientific testing" movement was entangled in racism and linguicism (Wiley, 1996, p. 60).

In response to such testing and resulting curriculum practices, in the mid-20th century, there were many educators who argued against this restrictive and functional approach to the teaching of reading. They believed that students should be able to read, understand, and critique literature, but not just the canons prevalent during the recitation era. Such educators favored the ideas postulated by John Dewey "who advocated a social, civic literacy based on democratic transactions and aimed toward democratic participation and solutions to social problems" (Myers, 1996, p. 85). In this spirit, many progressive educators, including Rousseau, Mann, and Parker advocated for making a more "meaningful connection between the immediate experiences of children and the organized knowledge of the disciplines" (Rippa, 1988, p. 187).

Progressive educators advocated for the inclusion of literature by emerging American authors such as Edgar Allan Poe, Walt Whitman, Mark Twain, Emily Dickinson, and others. This literature reflected the common speech and included a more common American voice. Thus, there was a distinction made between *reading instruction*, that is reading for information and *English instruction*, reading for the experience of engaging texts (Goodman, 1986).

However, the functional approach had the strongest support of administrators and politicians who deemed that the school curriculum needed to be centralized and consistent. At the same time, Dewey (1944) advocated student experience as central to the teaching-learning process, which contrasted scientific approaches that were too narrowly focused on the training of intellectual facilities as separate from the human experience.

Although there were many models of progressive schools, the scientific approach gained the most support in the early 20th century. In the elementary schools, children were taught to read using basal readers produced by curriculum reading experts utilizing a decoding method of instruction, with students grouped according to reading ability (Luke, 1988; Kelly, 1997). In the high schools, book lists were generated as to what literature could be read at certain grade and ability levels. Such instructional methodologies further reinforced the concept of *tracking*, where students were grouped together according to ability. "These tracks and courses sorted students inside schools, creating within the school program inequalities in race, ethnicity, social class, and gender" (Myers, 1996, p. 89). Apparently the goal of instruction during the early to mid-20th century was to model schooling as a factory, where the intent was to educate students as efficiently as possible. This in turn would assist in meeting the needs of the industrial workplace. According to a publication from the National Association Department of Superintendents in 1911,

> a basic reader is really one part of a system for teaching reading. This system includes the basic books themselves, the workbooks that go with them, and the teachers' manual, which tells what to do with the textbooks, what to do with the workbooks, and also tells all the other activities a teacher should go through in order to do a complete job of teaching reading" (Goodman et al., 1988, pp. 20–21).

To achieve such control, textbook publishers hired reading experts, who were intent on implementing the scientific approach to reading instruction. Such experts gave legitimacy to both the materials, and more importantly, to this approach to reading instruction (Coles, 1998; Taylor, 1998). Also in the high school, where students read literature, reading lists were made and distributed by boards of education and school administrators. In addition, publishers produced readers that included points for analysis and questions to determine comprehension. It follows then that discussion was controlled and guided by the experts, not by student or teacher interest or curiosity. Further, much of the control of the content and methods of teaching was stripped from teachers by the economic-minded administration, which was a direct reflection of the industrial market-ideology that overshadowed educational policy for much of this period (Apple, 1986), and appears to be reemerging in our present era.

As a result, the literacy of reading for information, decoding, and the writing of composition reflected the norm, so any other form of the past literacy periods was not deemed legitimate. The literacies of the past, which reflected natural processes of oracy, drawing, and inventive spelling, were seen not only as inappropriate, but incorrect. The decoding method, informed by scientific research and supported by industry and government, became the one standard form that could be taught and measured systematically for ultimate accountability (Shannon, 1989; Myers, 1996). This approach however, had little regard for student voice, critique, creativity, or uniqueness of the individual. Ralph Ellison addresses this issue in 1964 when he writes:

> the way to teach new forms or varieties or patterns of language is not to attempt to eliminate the old forms but to build upon them while at the same time valuing them in a way that is consonant with the desire for dignity that lies in each of us. Thus, if we deny or take away a student's language, we deny and diminish a crucial aspect of the student who uses it (cited in Riessman, 1976, p. 26).

It is important to note that by the 1940s, there was little credence given to reading for meaning or critical thinking, for "in the most common reading programs: beginning reading started with a basic sight vocabulary, after which came instruction in phonics and other word-analysis skills, then work with increasingly longer stories" (Coles, 1998, p. 57). However, in response to the political pressures of the Civil Rights movement beginning in the 1950s, with a public focus on educational equality, a shift or return to the progressive ideals began to emerge, and in the 1960s there was an emergence of a view that learning to read was a natural process where, children, in their own way and for their own reasons, "learn so much more rapidly and effectively than we could possibly teach them, that we can afford to throw away our curricula and our timetables, and set them free, at least most of the time to learn on their own" (Holt, 1967, p. 107). This reformulation helped inspire the reform known as *open education* aimed at breaking down the rigid structure and preset curricula of classrooms (Coles, 1998).

According to this theoretical model, teachers would provide students with materials including vocabulary words, talking points, listening tasks, writing prompts, and reading materials that they could access through their own processes, which were ultimately only facilitated by the teacher, and as a result of such processes children would learn how to read (Edelsky, Altwerger, & Flores, 1991; Coles, 1998). Thus, the other end of the pendulum was clearly defined, and this was the beginning of what has been now called the great debate, between the phonics approach (sound-symbol) and the process approach to literacy. During most of the 1960s and 1970s, whole-language processes gained in popularity; however the majority of instruction still reflected phonic skill approaches, which reflected the changing politics of the times (Coles, 1998; Taylor, 1998).

Another impact of the industrial model of literacy education that could   not be ignored was that functional processes did little to foster critical and higher-order thinking skills; skills that were fast becoming a requirement in the workplace (Murnane & Levy, 1996). In response, a shift took place early in the 1980s—not only in the workplace, where tasks were becoming more automated and workers were being replaced by technology, but also in the type of literacy instruction present in schools. National attention would be brought to the issues of education and literacy in the 1983 National Commission on Excellence in Education report, "*A Nation at Risk: The Imperative for Educational Reform.*" In the early 1980s the pendulum had started its long, slow arc back toward an earlier ideological standard, reflecting a process approach to literacy.

At the same time the nation was moving toward a definition of literacy standards, attitudes toward bilingual education were also beginning to shift from the restrictive policies, which were at their height from the 1920s through the 1940s. This is seen in the rate of decline of non-English languages in the United States, which is unprecedented for any country. Hakuta (1986) points out that in most nations it takes 350 years to replace non-native languages with dominant tongues; in the United States this process of language change took only one generation. For example, when citing the work of Lieberson, Dalto, and Johnston, Hakuta (1986) states that

> in 1940, 53 percent of the second-generation white Americans reported English as their mother tongue; in their parents' generation, only 25 percent had English as their mother tongue (p. 166).

So, just as the progressive idealists for literacy instruction were working to move policy toward a more student-centered, holistic curriculum, so too was there opportunity for shifts in policy toward the educational needs of language minority students.

Bilingual Education: The Period of Opportunity

> *The bilingual education program, often only a language program, was rarely integrated into either the philosophy of the practice of the school or of society. Its fate, therefore, was contingent upon political pressure* (Kanoon, 1978, p. 23).

> *The major forces shaping bilingual/bicultural educational policy — the forces that will largely determine not only its ultimate configuration, but more importantly, the role that bilingual/bicultural education will play in shaping a future for American society — are predominantly political rather than educational* (Burke, 1981, p. 165).

The movement from restrictive bilingual educational policies to policies of opportunity is in fact a reflection of the political shifts that began to occur in the United States beginning in the 1950s and 1960s. The National Defense and Education Act of 1958 was the first of many policies that started the shift from intolerance to more openness toward linguistic diversity (Kanoon, 1978). This legislation supported the teaching of foreign languages within public schools and universities. However, this policy was geared toward English speakers learning another language.

> From the 1920s until the 1960s little attention was given to the language needs of non-English-speaking students. Students were placed in regular classrooms, where they "sank or swam." It was not until the 1960s that the failure of English classrooms to educate non-English-speaking students began to receive national attention (Malakoff and Hakuta, 1990, p. 30).

This attention toward bilingual education occurred at the same time the Civil Rights movement was gaining momentum, with a focus on cultural pluralism and equal educational opportunity. The political movement transpired from assimilation toward ethnic and cultural pride. In 1963 Cuban exiles living in Dade County, Florida, established the first bilingual program in the United States since the 1920s, where the goal of instruction was for students to become biliterate in Spanish and English. This program was not only a great success but gained national recognition. In fact, the dual-language model that started at Coral Way Elementary School was so successful that similar programs were implemented in other elementary and middle schools within the state and across the nation (Malakoff & Hakuta, 1990; Brisk, 1998; Crawford, 1999).

The move toward bilingual programming occurred at the same time "the U.S. Congress set a minimum standard for the education of language minority students with Title VI of the 1964 Civil Rights Act, prohibiting discrimination on the grounds of race, color, or national origin in programs or activities receiving federal assistance" (Wiese & Garcia, 1998, p. 3). Thus, the issue of civil rights, which was "initially dominated by the demands and subsequent political remedies surrounding the issues of racial discrimination, elicited a heightened awareness of ethnic solidarity to which our political and educational institutions have been forced to respond" (Burke, 1981, pp. 165–166). By the time the Bilingual Education Act of 1968 was passed, other cities had created bilingual schools. For example, "in isolated communities in Arizona, California, Florida, New Mexico, Texas, and New Jersey, educators and parents created bilingual education programs to improve the education of their children" (Brisk, 1998, p. 8).

The Bilingual Education Act, Title VII of the Elementary and Secondary Education Act of 1965, set the policy guidelines for local school districts in states concerning the education of language minority students (Crawford, 1999). Within two years of this legislation, "twenty-one states had bilingual education programs concerned with Spanish, French, and Portuguese languages" (Kanoon, 1978, p. 23). In 1971, Massachusetts took the lead as the first of 21 states to implement a policy of mandatory bilingual education programs for language minority students. These bilingual programs varied from those in Dade County and other programs developed in the early 1960s as they utilized transitional rather than dual-language models wherein the students' native-language rather than being maintained to promote biliteracy, was utilized as a bridge to English (Baker, 1996). These new programs, while appearing to be progressive in nature, were not reflective of the initial intent of Title VII, enacted to provide funds for the creation of bilingual programs that supported the use a child's native language for initial, academic instruction and to teach English as a second language. Thus, the legislation that was enacted replaced the goal of native language and English development with that of making students proficient in English only. As Brisk (1998) and others have noted, the native language was used only to facilitate the acquisition of English, while further development and maintenance of the students' native language was not encouraged (Burke, 1981; August & Garcia, 1988; Malakoff & Hakuta, 1990; Baker, 1996). The result of varied programs with goals ranging from full bilingualism, to language maintenance, to the learning of English only, is reflected in the ambiguity of this ambitious legislation, which failed to articulate clearly three important considerations.

> First, the Act and the enabling regulations are not specific as to whether a funded bilingual education program should help maintain the language and culture of the minority group or if it should serve as a transition into the English-speaking classroom. Second, the Act did not specify when and for how long each language should be used. Third, the Act did not specify the criteria for selecting program participants (Behuniak et al., 1988, p. 485).

These ambiguities of policy can be seen in the variety of bilingual education programs that were implemented following this legislation, as the differences in programming reflected a difference in interpretation of the goals. What occurred is that programs primarily intended to develop students' English-language skills differed greatly from programs that were designed to facilitate acquisition of a foreign language (i.e., Spanish, French) by students who spoke the majority language of English (Behuniak et al., 1988). Thus, foreign-language instruction to majority English speakers was seen as adding to the students native language, while the teaching of English as a new language to bilingual students was seen as subtracting or replacing the students' native language with English.

During this period, bilingual programs, as depicted in Table 2, were either compensatory (viewing a student's ability in English as a deficit) or quality (viewing a student's native language as an asset). This difference of interpretation, at the policy level, is coupled with issues related to educational equity, access, and cultural pluralism (Espinosa & Ochoa, 1995). The real result of this dichotomy and the ambiguous policy was taken to the U.S. Supreme Court in 1974 with the *Lau v. Nichols* case. This lawsuit was filed on behalf of Chinese students in San Francisco who were failing in school because they could not understand the language of instruction. This case was taken to the Supreme Court because the state ruled that there was no segregation or disparate treatment of these students. The ruling of the state of California was, "if the Chinese children had a language deficiency, that was unfortunate, but the district was not to blame" (Crawford, 1999, p. 44). However, Justice Douglas held that "there is no equality of treatment merely by providing students with the same facilities, textbooks, teachers, and curriculum; for students who do not understand English are effectively foreclosed from any meaningful education " (Crawford, 1999, p. 566).

While "*Lau v. Nichols* did not require a particular instructional approach, it did establish the right of students to differential treatment based on their language minority status" (Wiese & Garcia, 1998, p. 3). This court case set precedent for policy and practice of bilingual education for years to come, most specifically through the Lau remedies, which were guidelines, not mandates, provided to school districts for implementing education programs for language minority students. These guidelines provided

> instructions for the identification, assessment, and mainstreaming of students. They suggested program options and standards for teacher preparation and recommended bilingual education as the best approach for elementary education, suggesting a number of approaches for the high school level (Brisk, 1998, p. 9).

Subsequently, these guidelines led to federal funding for program development and evaluation of the Title VII reauthorization. Bilingual education programs started to spread across the country and included models from dual language to transitional, while also providing funding for ESL and English tutoring in conjunction with native-language instruction (Wiese & Garcia, 1998; Crawford, 1999). This progressive movement is reflective of the literacy policy of whole-language instruction that was gaining popularity during the same time period in language arts and English classrooms in schools. However, as with most progressive movements in literacy, this movement toward equity in bilingual education began to move toward a more functional interpretation in the 1980s as the politics of the Right, where conservative agendas prevailed, returned.

Literacy and Bilingual Education Policy: 1960 to the Present

Transition to a New Standard of Literacy

> *Our dominant form of literacy is always the product of an explicit public debate and contention, often an unacknowledged one. And the choices between one form of literacy and another are frequently implicit in other decisions, often located in obscure resolutions of technological, economic, and political differences. Finally of course, the ultimate consensus is not the only one possible* (Myers, 1996, p. 102).

From the 1960s through the 1980s, urban school populations became more diverse and the needs of the workplace began to change, both of which had a direct influence on the nation's definition of standards of literacy. In the 1930s minimum literacy was defined as three or more years of school; in the 1940s it was raised to a 4th-grade reading ability. In 1952 it was at the 6th-grade level, and then in 1970 it was suggested that functional literacy was now reading at a 12th-grade level. However, literacy skills on this continuum were limited to a decoding/ analytic definition of literacy and only involved measuring what students could actually read or decode, and negated all previous literacy forms, most noticeably oral (i.e., community and cultural discourse patterns) and signature forms (i.e., drawing, inventive spelling) (Myers, 1996). This functional view of literacy is reflected in the 1960 UNESCO definition of a literate person:

> A person is literate when he has acquired essential knowledge and skills which enable him to engage in all those activities in which literacy is required for effective functioning in his group or community, and whose attainment of reading, writing and arithmetic make it possible for him to continue to use these skills toward his own and the community's development (International Committee of Experts on Literacy Report, UNESCO, Paris, 1962, cited in McKay, 1993, p. 4).

This definition, while acknowledging literacy as knowledge, emphasizes the use of written forms with the goal of community development. Thus, this worldview of literacy is mostly concerned with the act of reading and not with the full engagement of text, including voice, questioning, and going beyond the text or *word* to *world* (Freire & Macedo, 1987).

Functional approaches to literacy began to prove problematic in the 1970 and into the 1980s. It was during this time that a study by the National Assessment of Educational Progress (NAEP) determined that

"72 percent of seventeen-year-olds could correctly answer literacy comprehension items, but that these same students were not prepared to undertake explanatory tasks, problem-solving strategies or critical thinking" (Myers, 1996, p. 109). Such limited skills were deemed inadequate as technology not only began to emerge, but became part of school and society, a place where students ultimately would need to have the skills and capacity to critique, interpret, and translate intentions and meaning behind words in texts. One other important factor that contributed to this need for new standards was the change in demographics within our society and the related needs of personal growth and empowerment (Myers, 1996). Thus, new literacy standards were beginning to be examined that included student participation and voice in the process of learning to read. Whole-language and constructivist teaching/learning models emerged and gained popularity in response to the analytic definition of literacy. Such methodologies were based on the democratic principles advocated first by Dewey (1904), where students' language is valued and is part of the curriculum, and by current educational researchers such as F. Smith (1971), K. Goodman, (1986) and others (Shannon, 1990; Routmann, 1994; Coles, 1998; Weaver, 1998). These researchers contend that all language processes inform literate development, that is,

> in a whole language perspective, it is not just oral language that counts as language. Oral language, written language, sign language—each of these is a system of linguistic conventions for creating meanings. That means none is the basis for the other; none is a secondary representation of the other. It means that *whatever* is language is learned like language and acts like language. While each mode (oral, written, sign) has its own set of constraints and opportunities, they all share certain characteristics: (1) they are profoundly social; (2) they contain interdependent and inseparable subsystems; and (3) they are predictable (Edelsky, Altwerger, & Flores, 1991, pp. 9–10).

In the early to mid- 1980s, whole-language methods were becoming the core of most literate classroom instruction and changed the focus from technical instruction of reading, to literacy as a more natural process, allowing children choice in reading materials, where teachers utilized literature and authentic materials rather than basal texts. In addition, students were encouraged to respond both orally and in writing to literature and text based on their own experiences; to critique texts; to question the author's message; analyze characters plots, and themes of stories; and to extend meaning in their own writing processes (Hobson & Shuman, 1990; Myers, 1996; Courts, 1997; Coles, 1998).

It turned out that this new, more progressive standard was short-lived. Toward the mid-1980s, the movement for a return to basics and the need for a defined cultural literacy were reemerging with strong political support. In 1983 the National Commission on Excellence in Education published *A Nation at Risk: The Imperative for Educational Reform*, which like the recent No Child Left Behind Act, had a direct impact on education and made literacy "a front-burner issue, achieving a prominence unseen since the panic over Sputnik" (Crawford, 1999, p. 229). This report was promoted by the conservative groups and the media and focused the nation's attention on the failure of schools and the need to define clearer educational standards and accountability measures (Apple, 1995; Ravitch, 1995):

> Education reform became a site of ideological conflict, as conservatives saw an opportunity to advance their agenda ... Politicians on the Right articulated a critique that made sense to frustrated parents. They drew connections between declining test scores, innovations like whole language and the "new math", child centered approaches that de-emphasized rote learning, and moral relativist, as exemplified by sex education and the ban on school prayer. They had no trouble identifying the enemy: the "educational establishment" portrayed as a bureaucratic leviathan dependent on big government and loyal to its liberal social agenda (Crawford, 1999, p. 229).

The consequences for literacy education, then as now, were an increase in phonics and basic-skill programs and a decrease in whole-language and student-centered approaches (Myers, 1996; Taylor, 1998). The societal factors that contributed to this movement to the Right were the growing diversity of students and the schools' failure to meet the needs of this growing urban population. During this time, schools were becoming overcrowded with classes in many inner-city schools exceeding 35 students, taking place in school gyms, and inside decaying buildings. There was a stark difference between the conditions at inner-city schools and those in white suburbs, which tended to be more modern with smaller class sizes (Kozol, 1991).

This new standard of functional ideology promoted the use of ability grouping, or tracking, to teach students how to read. This approach, still present in many high schools, while intended to sort students according to reading levels, in effect sorts them according to race and class. This movement toward a more conservative agenda had a great impact on bilingual education as well. It was at this time that federal funding went to more transitional programs, with the goal to teach English over native language.

Bilingual Education: The Dismissive Period, 1980s to the Present

When the Bilingual Education Act, Title VII, was reauthorized in 1978, it stated that native languages should be used only to the extent necessary for a child to achieve competence in English. It resulted in programs that shifted from dual language and maintenance toward submersion and transitional bilingual education (Baker, 1996; Brisk, 1998; Crawford, 1999). According to the guidelines, federal funds could not be used for maintenance programs. Further, in 1984 and 1988, funds were increasingly available to programs where a student's first language was *not* used. Such funding policies are reflective of the conservative politics of the times. In 1981, then President of the United States, Ronald Reagan, stated:

> It is absolutely wrong and against the American concept to have a bilingual education program that is now openly, admittedly, dedicated to preserving their native language and never getting them adequate in English so they can go out into the job market and participate (cited in Crawford, 1999, p. 53).

Also in 1981, a federally funded review of bilingual programs by Adriana de Kanter and Keith Baker resulted in the publication of a government report that stated: "There exists insufficient evidence to prove that bilingual education is the most effective approach for language minority children." In addition, the report "called for English immersion as the solution to the 'language problem'" (cited in Ochoa & Caballero-Allen, 1988, p. 20) and tended to support "one branch of public opinion in the United States that saw bilingual education as failing to foster integration" (Baker, 1996, p. 211). It concluded that the federal government should not legislate or advocate any particular education program (Ochoa & Caballero-Allen, 1988; Baker, 1996). So the conclusion is, rather than continue to develop programs that follow "the common sense observation that children should be taught in a language they understand," schools should develop programs that teach English using good teaching strategies in order to ensure achievement in both English and content subject matter simultaneously while ensuring that the subject matter is not taught ahead of the language. Further, it was believed that since "the language minority child must ultimately function in an English speaking society," then schools should be responsible for providing "second language instruction in all subjects," which in the end may be preferable to bilingual methods (Baker & de Kanter cited in Baker, 1996, p. 212).

Thus, the government review was a reflection of the sentiment of the majority opinion and "the dominant government preference for English-only and transitional bilingual education" (Baker, 1996) and failed to engage educational research on dual language or language maintenance programs and, as such, reflects ideological positions not related to sound pedagogy and practice (Ochoa & Caballero-Allen, 1988; Baker, 1996). So, "coexisting with the contradiction between politics and pedagogy are differences over ends and means: What should the schools be teaching LEP children, and how should it be taught?" (Crawford, 1992, p. 314). Unfortunately the Bilingual Education Act of 1968 left such issues ambiguous and unresolved, and set the stage for the ultimate dismantling of bilingual education programs that has occurred in many states across the country.

As a result of unmandated government policy and government-funded research in the 1980s led to more funding for transitional program models, the number of transitional programs grew while maintenance and dual-language programs decreased (Ochoa & Caballero-Allen, 1988). Presently, most immigrant students identified as LEP in middle and high schools receive a portion of instruction in English as Second Language (ESL) or English Language Development (ELD) classes, where much of the focus of instruction is the development of basic interpersonal communicative skills (BICS) and literacy skills deemed necessary for success in monolingual English classrooms. In addition, LEP students receive specially designed academic instruction in English (SDAIE) where they have the opportunity to develop their cognitive academic language proficiency (CALP) through content area instruction (Cummins, 1994). However, the theoretical framework supporting these language programs emphasizes maintenance and development of primary language (L1) while supporting a transition to English (L2) based on a model of language empowerment. The sad reality is that these authentic, democratic ideologies and empowering teaching pedagogies are diminished with an overt focus on assisting students in acquiring English as rapidly as possible. As in the restrictive policies of the past, movement toward more standardized and narrow forms of literacy and bilingual education are motivated out of public opinion and fear of foreigners rather than on issues related to educational equity and cultural pluralism (Crawford, 1992; Horton & Calderon, 1992; Montaner, 1992; Krashen, 1994; Crawford, 1999; Escobedo, 1999; Macedo et al., 2003).

Presently there are approximately 3 million LEP students in the United States, with California public schools being home to more than 1.4 million. This number represents 45% of all LEP students nation-wide (California Department of Education, 2002), with 40% of this total being Spanish speakers (Snow, 2000). At the state level, California has responded to this increase of LEP students through two legislative pro-posals that not only impact educational policy and programming, but have received nationwide attention and controversy. These proposals were in the form of voter ballot initiatives. The first, Proposition 187, was designed to prevent undocumented immigrants from receiving public services, including public school education (Adams, 1995; Escobedo, 1999). The second and most recent was Proposition 227, titled "English for the Children," which called for the elimination of bilin-gual education and required all public school students identified as LEP to be taught "overwhelmingly" in English (Escobedo, 1999; Kerper-Mora, 2000a).

The first of these two measures, Proposition 187, passed in 1994 with over 60% of voter support. Ultimately, implementation of the mea-sure was stopped by legal challenges in both state and federal courts on the grounds of civil rights violations (Escobedo, 1999). Of signifi-cance, the fact that this measure had such strong public support is an indicator of the "climate of reprisal and fear for Latino immigrant fami-lies and their children in our schools" (Escobedo, 1999, p. 14). Adams (1995) points out that this public opinion is reflected in the voting popu-lation, not the population as a whole. It is amazing to imagine that even if every potentially eligible person of color were registered and voted in concert with the 77% Latino "no" vote, Prop. 187 would still have passed (Adams, 1995). Unfortunately the voter proposition process has forced the election process across the country to become a space where "voters express their disaffection, their alienation, and their fears, rather than their hopes, visions, or aspirations" (Adams, 1995, p. 17).

This sentiment could not be truer, as seen when Proposition 227 was introduced only four years later in 1998. Proposition 227, "English for the Children," passed with 61% voter approval. The goals of this proposition are to "teach English as rapidly as possible, by heavily ex-posing ELLs to English; to reduce drop out rates among immigrants; and, to reverse low literacy rates and promote economic and social ad-vancement for language minority students" (Kerper-Mora, 2000a). This proposition does not deny bilingual education, but doesn't make it readily accessible either. Proposition 227 states that "alternatives to this proscriptive program [structured English immersion] may be provided pursuant to the initiative's 'parental exception waiver' provisions. These waivers can only be provided with prior written consent and are only available subject to certain prescribed criteria" (Escobedo, 1999, p. 15). In response to this, schools and districts in California created parental waivers so that those schools that had bilingual programs could maintain them, and parents who elected to have their children in bilingual education could do so (Escobedo, 1999; Kerper-Mora, 2000b).

Interestingly, the anti-bilingual sentiment in this proposition is not unlike that revealed in the government report, cited previously by Baker and de Kanter in 1983. According to Kerper-Mora, (2000b), the reasoning provided by proponents of 227 to discount bilingual education is expressed in the language of the law itself, citing that

> Bilingual education is the reason for low levels of English proficiency among immigrant students, especially Latinos who are the group served by the vast majority of the bilingual programs. Bilingual education slows down the English language acquisition process or prevents English language learners from becoming fully proficient in English. Therefore, bilingual education contributes to the high dropout rates among Latinos. Since bilingual education is the problem, getting rid of it is the solution (Kerper-Mora, 2000b).

Since the passage of this proposition and other similar measures in other states, the majority of ELLs have been placed in programs identified as structured English immersion. These programs are subtractive in nature, where "the learning of a majority second language may undermine a person's minority first language and culture, thus creating a subtractive situation" (Baker, 1996, p. 66). Within this dismissive period of bilingual education, this subtractive model is gaining strength within the policy arena as the number of English-language learners in schools increase across the country. Additionally, other states, including Arizona and more recently Massachusetts (the site of the first public mandated bilingual programs in the United States), have adopted even more restrictive measures than Proposition 227. Within one year, virtually all bilingual education programs in Arizona and Massachusetts were being dismantled and replaced with a compensatory education model of structured English immersion.

Bridging the Future

Viewing literacy as the ability to read and write wrongly places literacy in the individual, rather than in the society of which that person is a member. As such it obscures the multiple ways in which reading, writing and language interrelate with the workings of power and desire in social life (Gee, 1990, p. 27).

Policies such as Propositions 187 and 227 value cultural and linguistic conformity over cultural plurality and linguistic diversity (Crawford, 1999; Escobedo, 1999; Kerper-Mora, 2000b). They reflect, and more importantly, promote the impact that public opinion and public policy have on teaching and pedagogy. Accordingly, English learners are viewed as having a *problem*, thus equating a student's lack of English as a deficit, which results in a compensatory education model versus a quality education model as depicted in Table 2. Within a compensatory frame, the education of students is deemed possible only in English without recognizing the value of native language abilities and knowledge (Brisk, 1998); "schools in the United States have all too often operated under a "deficit" model of learning which (implicitly or explicitly) endorses the rejection of the home culture in favor of generic, American culture" (Matthews, 2000). A compensatory model further perpetuates a functional and cultural ideology toward literacy education that is both simplistic and reductionistic in terms of approach, methodology, and curricula (McKay, 1993; McLaren, 1998). As such, a critical examination of the policies for programming for literacy and language learning needs to be addressed by those who are most impacted by the policy decisions—teachers (Aronowitz & Giroux, 1985; Apple, 1986; Macedo, 1994)—because, as this review has indicated, much of the public policy for literacy and bilingual education has and continues to be connected deeply to political concerns. In order to challenge such policies and become true advocates for our students, we as teachers must begin to examine not only how literacy is defined, but how it is contextualized within very particular sociopolitical movements. As this review has shown, and Baker (1996) points out, "history shows that there is constant change, a constant movement in ideas, ideology, and impetus" (p. 171) for educational policies. Such changes are brought about by educational researchers, teachers, and citizens who are willing to engage in the ongoing discussions and debates surrounding the crucial topics of our times.

This chapter establishes a clear framework for identifying and analyzing language policy along ideological and political-historical positions. It can be seen that teaching curriculum and methods, which constitute the common language for teachers, and which are often engaged in apolitical and ahistorical terms, are not only political and historical, but ideological in nature. However, before engaging and examining the connections between policy and teaching practice, which make up Part II of this book, we will first consider two concepts of critical theory that are necessary in taking up critical dialogue and reflection, those of historicity of knowledge and hegemony. Without a clear understanding of how our own histories are informed and taken up within public spaces in our democratic, capitalistic society, a true critical analysis of present teacher practice cannot be fully engaged.

Reflective Activity: Using Table 3, the Framework for Examining Policy & Programming for English Language Learners, examine the policy and programs for English language learners from the policy levels of the state, county, city, and school where you presently work or the community in which you live, and the stakeholder perspectives of the administrators and program coordinators.

1) Consider how each group identifies or defines the following elements of programming: value for learners, literacy orientation, instructional goals, resources, accountability assessment, expectations for learners, and program approaches and how they reflect the ideologies presented here.

2) Consider how the programs value bilingual education as either compensatory or quality, and how the literacy curriculum is either in concert with that view or varies from it. You will notice in Table 3 that not all stakeholders are considered. The elements of curriculum, teachers, students, and parents are highlighted, but left out in order to place the focus on what is imposed or programmed. At the end of Chapter 6 you will have an opportunity to revisit this table and your notes to consider these other key stakeholders.

Table 3: Framework for Examining Policy & Programming for English Language Learners

ELL/Bilingual Policy	Value for Learners	Literacy Orientation	Instructional Goals	Resources	Accountability and Assessment	Expectations for Learners	Program Approaches
Federal							
State							
County							
School District							
School Site							
STAKEHOLDERS							
Administrator							
Program Coordinator							
Teachers & Curriculum							
Students & Parents							

- **Value for Learners:** Examines how ELLs are viewed within the policy and program and by concerned stakeholders (i.e., teachers, administrators, parents, self). Areas of concentration include learners as valued participants in the learning process, value for being bilingual, biliterate, or learning English.

- **Literacy Orientation:** Addresses various definitions of literacy among stakeholders. Areas of concern here include the value that is placed on literacy as well as recognition for various forms of literacy and language learning. Essentially how is literacy valued, not only among teachers and students but across policy and programs. This dimension seeks to clarify the multiple forms of literacy that are important and valued by stakeholders

- **Instructional Goals:** Identifies the goal of instruction and learning and the expectation in relation to learning English and Content.

- **Resources:** Identifies the financial and human resources that are allocated/dedicated to programming and curricula for ELLs. Included here are personnel resources such as capacity of teaching staff and materials utilized in curriculum development and teaching.

- **Accountability and Assessment:** Determines accountability of not only student achievement and success, but program implementation such as transition and testing, as well as the accountability levels of those responsible for the process.

- **Expectations for Learners:** Clarifies expectations of students as defined by the stakeholders and policy and programs. For example, by graduation what are students expected to be able to do and/or accomplish, including expectations and methods of preparedness.

- **Program Approaches:** Examines the multiple programs presently utilized or engaged within classrooms and schools. Program models most often found at the secondary level include: Specially Designed Academic Instruction in English (SDAIE), English as a Second Language (ESL), and Transitional Bilingual. Each program approach can then be evaluated across the six dimensions above. The core concern here is, how does program approach(es) support or interact with literacy orientation, instructional goals, resources, accountability/assessment, and expectations for learners.

Chapter 3
Engaging Factors of Hegemony & Historicity of Knowledge

Each society has its regime of truth, its "general politics" of truth: that is the types of discourse which it accepts and makes function as true; the mechanisms and instances which enable one to distinguish true and false statements; the means by which each is sanctioned; the techniques and procedures accorded value in the acquisition of truth; the status of those who are charged with saying what counts is true (Foucault, 1977, p. 131).

The rationale for having school curriculum is derived from the Common School Movement of the 1800s. The belief of this movement was (and still is) that schooling children would benefit the greater society by: (a) socializing children of different social, ethnic, and religious backgrounds to coexist peacefully; (b) teaching children the skills and habits of the workplace, thus reducing crime and poverty; and (c) encouraging all children to value patriotism by fostering the idea of democracy as the best political system (Pinar, Reynolds, Slattery, & Taubman, 1996). In doing this, it was believed, public schools would accomplish the major task of "producing citizens with a common core of knowledge who think of themselves as patriotic Americans and who can be financially independent of the state" (Hinchey, 1998, p. 13).

It is interesting to note the language used in stating the three goals of schooling. The word "teach" is overtly used when referring to the development of skills and habits. While the remaining goals imply a covert process; the action of *teaching* is not articulated, but rather implied by stating that students will be *socialized* and *encouraged*. These actions are more powerful and pervasive because they permeate an individual's belief system. This is accomplished by curriculum materials made available to schools, which then become the mechanism that supports the achievement of the goals articulated by the school curriculum.

It is easy to see that the manner in which knowledge becomes legitimatized in schools is through textbooks: "whether we like it or not, the curriculum in most American schools is not defined by courses of study or suggested programs, but by one particular artifact, the standardized grade-level specific text" (Apple, 1986, p. 85). Further, "School textbooks—despite the historical development of an anonymous authoritative 'textbookese' which succeeds in disguising their subjective and ideological origins—remain commodities, objects produced and consumed by human subjects" (Luke, 1988, p. 64). An examination of the historical context of the literacy curricula reveals how textbooks, reading materials, and instruction function in supporting specific political and ideological agendas and making certain knowledg *legitimate* while appropriating certain literacies in order to perpetuate and sustain societal distinctions based on race and class (Freire & Macedo, 1987; Apple, 1986). While the purpose of this text is not to examine textbooks in particular, it is necessary to consider how we as teachers and educators engage, adopt, and teach from certain texts, including this one.

In this chapter we will consider two main concepts of critical theory that support such an interrogation: first, hegemony, the unquestioning acceptance of societal goals and second, historicity of knowledge, an individual's or group's historical perspective. These concepts are tools utilized by critical theorists to engage critique and questioning of theory, practice, and pedagogy. According to Shor (1992), "a curriculum that avoids questioning school and society is not, as it is commonly supposed, politically neutral" (p. 12). The premise here is that most middle- and upper-class parents of the dominant culture, as well as most educators, would agree that public schools and the literacy curriculum in particular serve to teach our children how to read, write, and speak about our country's culturally important historical subjects. These ideals include democracy, equal opportunity, and equal rights and are currently represented in most curriculum textbooks. Most parents would also agree that schools tend to place a high value on obeying the teacher, following rules, learning basic skills, and being a good citizen; through schools, students become immersed in a particular school culture, which then supports the immersion into national culture (Hinchey, 1998; Giroux, 1996). So the question now becomes, how do we, as teachers, come to believe these accepted norms and then adapt them to practice?

Hegemony

The key to winning, to establishing hegemony, is usually that group which can establish the parameters of the terms of the debate, that group which can incorporate the competing claims of other groups under its own discourse about education and social goals (Apple, 1986, pp. 26–27).

Hegemony is "the power of one class to articulate the interest of the other social groups to its own" (Mouffe, 1979, p. 183). In Gramsci's view, hegemony not only imposes domination, but transforms beliefs, values, cultural traditions, and social practices, to perpetuate and make real the existing social order, that is, what we know as our *everyday*. In schools, such hegemony is systematically distributed through the selection of literacy materials and instructional practices determined by policy makers and school administrators, and then implemented by teachers in classrooms. As reflected here in the previous chapters and by other critical theorists (Aronowitz & Giroux, 1991; Darder, 1991; Macedo, 1994; Apple, 1996; Giroux, 1996; Kelly, 1997; McLaren, 1998), the practice and pedagogies of all literacies, in school and society, inherently reflect the political, social, and moral visions of the individuals and institutions that hold the majority of wealth and power in our society. In English classrooms across our country it can be found that the "literacy (curriculum) falsely suggests a set of practices that are univocal and generic, thereby denying literacies, the myriad ways in which seemingly generic skills are practiced—imported, adopted, adapted, and transformed within specific cultural frameworks" (Kelly, 1997, p. 8).

One example of such hidden or hegemonic factors is the use of ability grouping and tracking in junior and senior high school English classes. We all have seen or experienced these classes where students are assigned to classes based on standardized test scores, IQ, language fluency, and/or perceived abilities or disabilities, generalized to certain groups of students (Oakes, 1985). This hegemonic form is sometimes referred to as the *hidden curriculum* in that those who implement the system of tracking believe that students have a choice and that if students achieve then they can move up. The curriculum is hidden, as will be made clear in Chapter 5, in the sense that students, parents, and even teachers fail to see that ability grouping and tracking are not based on merit, but have become accepted through the "tacit teaching to students of norms, values, and dispositions that goes on simply by their living in, and coping with, the institutional expectations and routines of schools, day in and day out, for a number of years" (Apple, 1979, p. 14).

For example, in many junior and senior high schools I have visited during the last three years I observed students identified as poor readers or in need of skill development, learning to read through a variety of basal skills programs (i.e., the SRA program for Corrective Reading). The students who participate in these classes instead of grade level English classes are selected based on graded reading tests. If students score below the 25th percentile on this test or other state standardized measures, and are not identified as limited English proficient (LEP), they are placed in a school-adopted basal reading program. It was disconcerting but not surprising to see that the majority of students in these skill-based classes were from lower socioeconomic backgrounds, and ethnically and linguistically diverse. This practice then amounts to tracking in a district that states it does not track students, but advocates through its mission statement to:

> Provide an equitable, academic experience for students who have a home language other than English and to support the district's third goal, namely, to implement a flexible, student-centered course of study that will prepare students for the global, multilingual society of the 21st century and target bilingual skills. (Quote from Southern California High School District Mission Statement.)

However, a program such as the SRA Corrective Reading is designed to build necessary skills in reading in English in a very teacher-directed and teacher-centered manner. Within this program students are taught to read by responding in unison to clicks and scripted teacher directions. Thus, the hidden curriculum is one that prepares these students to respond to rules, teacher commands, and to complete many tasks that have only one correct response or answer. This form of hegemony is by far the most devastating, and on many levels dehumanizing, in that it not only separates students by race, class, culture, or language, it further fosters differing beliefs about self and others based on the content of the curriculum and the instructional practices it evokes (Oakes, 1985; Darder, 1991; Apple, 1996).

If such hegemony exists and the structures can and are identified, as above, how do we then engage in our own use of these district- and school-mandated curricula programs? That is, many of the readers of this text may have in the past or presently have experienced either being tracked, or teaching students using a program similar to Corrective Reading. So, how do we identify what it is we believe about effective student-centered practices for reading development that include student voice, language, and culture? What are best practices within a structure that advocates a specific curriculum program—that in many respects appears to be working? In order to do this we must first begin with our own historical knowledge, our learned understandings of the world and our own processes of becoming literate.

Such a process engages individuals in historicity of knowledge, where humans are viewed as historical beings that create knowledge (McLaren, 1998). This concept goes beyond learning in a traditional sense and values individuals and their own lived experiences as valid and valuable. Therefore, when engaging in critical inquiry where ideology is being defined, as in this text, it should be taken in light of the historical knowledge that is available to each of us as individuals. It is our own historical knowledge that should both challenge the notion of absolute truths, and highlight further the varying definitions, interpretations, and methods that truth holds for each of us. That is, the truth should not be "understood as a set of 'discovered laws' that exist outside power/knowledge relations [and] which somehow correspond with the real" (McLaren, 1998, p. 184), but should be taken in the context of not only world and cultural history, but community and personal histories.

So in this inquiry it is important to consider the *real* of each of us as individuals and as teachers. That is, we function in the world and in our classrooms informed both by professional and personal realities and experience. However, many of us have come to accept that our classroom reality is ahistorical rather than historical and ideological. Thus, engagement of literacy is informed not only from the historical context of the curriculum and related ideology, but the historical context of each one who participates in our classrooms. Critical educators define ideology as, "the production and representation of ideas, values, and beliefs" (McLaren, 1998, p. 180). Ideology as stated here both informs and values the knowledge of the individual, along with the knowledge we each present, represent, and re-present both in personal as well as professional interactions. To further address the need for personal examination of our lived realities, Pinar (2000) argues that to be fully engaged in curriculum we must establish ourselves as beings not apart from our personal histories or school experiences but through them. That is we need to truly engage the method of *currere*—the Latin infinitive of curriculum—"as a strategy for reconfiguring one's self, especially one's relationship to one's 'subject matter,' one's academic discipline, which is spiritual, psychological, and political discipline as well" (Pinar, 2000, p. 41). To begin this inquiry and illustrate this concept, I include here my personal/professional autobiography, and contextualize it as a form of an educational autobiography, illustrating the process of *currere*, which "seeks to enlarge and enliven the conversation—the highly specialized, bureaucratized, formalized conversation—that is the school curriculum" (Pinar, 2000, p. 41). The following illuminates the historical context I bring to my learning, teaching, and research processes as well as this very text. I will articulate my historical presence and then ask you, the reader, to explore your own educational autobiography in the form of *currere*, and to consider it in relation to or against mine, those of your peers, others reading this text, your professor, your students and their parents, and ultimately the curriculum. Once we begin to acknowledge, identify, and recognize our own historical contexts, we can be better prepared to engage notions of hegemony and political ideology, and more deeply and critically examine our teaching processes and related curriculum from a more holistic perspective. This then engages a critical ontological perspective that necessitates a movement "beyond mechanistic metaphors of selfhood" and "to appreciate that political empowerment, community-building, and the cultivation of both the individual and the collective intellect require a constant monitoring of the relationships that shape us" (Kincheloe, 2003, pp. 47–48) and our responses to curriculum pedagogy and policy.

Author Autobiographical Profile

I am a forty-five-year-old Euro-American white woman, born and raised with three siblings in a working-class neighborhood in a small New England town. Both of my parents had at least one parent who was an immigrant to the United States and had parents who spoke languages other than English; from the Azores in Portugal (father) and Quebec, Canada (mother). My parents didn't speak their respective parents' native languages, and both completed school to the 6th grade, having to leave school to help support their large families. While not high school educated, they placed a high value on education and the receipt of a high school diploma. So, as many of their generation and class did, they trusted the schools and teachers to provide appropriately for all their children.

In my sophomore year of high school I had been tracked as a low reader. This was determined by my performance on standardized test scores, and my lack of academic achievement in my previous grade-level English classes. As a result I was enrolled in mostly a phonics and skills-based literacy program for most of my remaining high school education. Although I enjoyed reading, and was an avid reader at home, I had few opportunities within the school environment to read literature, such as poetry and novels. I was impacted by this tracking, or hidden curriculum, by not receiving the appropriate curriculum to prepare me to attend college. When I inquired in my senior year of high school about taking the SATs, my counselor informed me that I had not taken the appropriate courses to prepare me for this test. I was told that maybe I could attend community college with some assistance, but the message I received was that college was not within my reach at that time and may never be if I didn't acquire the prerequisite knowledge, which was not given to me by my high school.

As a young adult I worked in a variety of service and factory jobs and later, in several office management positions. In addition to work, I traveled in the United States, Mexico, Europe, and Southeast Asia. I relocated to San Diego, California, in the early 1980s and during this time I had the opportunity to live in Kuala Lumpur, Malaysia, for a year (1984) and in Guadalajara, Mexico, for three months, (1988). In both of these foreign settings I needed to learn the verbal and cultural language of these communities in order to function appropriately. The success of language learning was forged through a combination of classroom instruction and community immersion.

Based on my varied life experiences I found my interests were connected to culture, language, and teaching. I began college at the age of 25 and five years later completed my BA in psychology and acquired my first teaching credential. In 1988 I started my teaching career, my first full-time position was as a special education teacher of students with communicative and developmental delays. Since then I have taught both elementary and high school special education classes for students with learning and emotional difficulties. The majority of my K–12 teaching experience has been with high school at-risk youth. In 1995, in addition to teaching at the high school level, I taught ESL at a local job training program and then went on to teach beginning-level ESL for nine years at a community college. I completed my Ph.D. in 2001 and now teach methods courses in a credential program for bilingual teachers, and Masters' courses in critical literacy and social justice.

As a K–12 teacher who taught in programs that functioned from a deficit model where the students were viewed as being deficient in reading and language production, I experienced the frustration of teaching and utilizing materials that did not match my beliefs about how students learn to read and write. I also saw my students as having strengths and capabilities, as well as languages and cultures, which were not acknowledged or represented in the school curriculum. Thus, my motivation for doing research in the area of teachers' ideology and literacy was to address issues of pedagogy and practice that impacted not only my own learning, but my teaching experiences. I wanted to engage in a process of research that validated teacher and student experiences without strictly compartmentalizing or evaluating methods, but examining processes and position. This I was able to accomplish in my dissertation research with a small group of teachers, in my university classes with student teacher candidates and experienced teachers, and now here in this text. So along with the literature I have read and reviewed, and my research with high school teachers of ELLs, the life experiences and positions I have held as a student, teacher, researcher, and author influence and inform my research, my teaching, and this text.

Reflective Activity: Take a moment to reflect on your own personal and school history, your beliefs, and informed knowledge. Before reading further, write your own personal profile. How you have come to know what you do in your teaching? What were your literacy learning experiences? How do these experiences influence your teaching? How do these experiences influence your ideology of literacy?

1) How do you relate to what has been presented in this text thus far?

2) Share your profile with a colleague or two and discuss the similarities and differences in how your histories inform both your personal and professional roles in life.

3) How do you understand or relate to the concept of hegemony?

Historicity of Knowledge

As you begin to examine your own personal history and path of understanding truth, you must also examine the contexts in which your reality or truth gets constructed. To begin the process of becoming a critical educator you must ask "how and why knowledge gets constructed the way it does, and how and why some constructions of reality are legitimated and celebrated by the dominant culture while others clearly are not" (McLaren, 1998, p. 174). Many critical education theorists, such as Willis, Giroux, and Freire, emphasize the moral imperative of education where we need to recognize our own human agency as part of the production of knowledge and culture. In doing this we also need to "take into account the power of material and ideological structures" (Weiler, 1988, p. 13). So we can't just look at our histories as personal stories that take place outside of school, the dominant culture, or power relations. Rather, as teachers and educators we need to examine how knowledge is connected to societal power relations and recognize that "knowledge is not simply what teachers teach, but also the productive meanings that students [as well as teachers] in all their cultural and social difference, bring to classrooms as part of the production of knowledge and the construction of personal and social identities" (Giroux, 1988, p. 162).

To put it simply, it is the recognition of agency and knowledge production that underlies the principle of historicity of knowledge. This principle is based on the idea that knowledge is not created in a vacuum, but is contextual, occurring through interactions with varying societal and environmental elements. Historicity of knowledge also views humans as historical beings who create knowledge; this concept then goes beyond learning in a traditional sense and values individuals and their own experiences. Finally, any historical knowledge should challenge the notion of absolute truths, definitions, interpretations, and methods and must not be "understood as a set of 'discovered laws' that exist outside power/knowledge relations and which somehow correspond with the real" (McLaren, 1998, p. 184), but within each of us as individuals who do not live in isolation from others, but with and through others and the greater society.

So how does this relate to how we view knowledge in the context of schools? Giroux (1988) points out that knowledge, specifically that derived from the curriculum, must be understood "as representative of a set of underlying interests that structure how a particular story is told through the organization of knowledge, social relations, values, and forms of assessment" (p. 165).   Thus, as critical educators we must be acutely aware of the ideology, defined as "the production and representation of ideas, values, and beliefs" (McLaren, 1998, p. 180), which informs not only our own knowledge, but the knowledge we carry, present, represent, and re-present to our children and students. So as a teacher I challenge you to consider the following statement:

> Knowledge is not produced in the intentions of those who believe they hold it
> .... It [knowledge] is produced in the process of interaction, between writer
> and reader at the moment of reading, and between teacher and learner at the
> moment of classroom engagement. Knowledge is not the matter that is offered
> so much as the matter that is understood (Lusted, 1986, pp. 4–5).

We can add one more element to the above, that is, to also understand knowledge in relation to the political and power relations that produce it and the traditions that inform and value a particular knowledge as "true," or more accurately, knowledge that is "legitimated both culturally and politically" by the dominant culture (Giroux, 1988, p. 164). Thus, knowledge becomes a critical element in reproduction and critical education theory in particular.

~~~~~~~~~~~~

Reflective Activity: At this point pause for a moment to refer back to the reflection you wrote on your own history, and consider how you have come to know certain truths or accept certain teaching materials, methods, or processes as being the most valid. How did you come to know this? What is your role as a transmitter of knowledge? What knowledge do you transfer to your students? How? More importantly, how do you construct and measure knowledge in your classroom?

~~~~~~~~~~~~

I believe that historicity of knowledge, although seemingly complex, is an important and necessary principle within critical education theory as it delves into the processes supporting the social structures that maintain and reproduce existing power relationships along with social, economic, and class structures. The task of critical educators, and the challenge I place before you, is to first examine the mechanisms of knowledge production and commodification. Second, be willing to participate in critical dialogue with others to address your own history, class context, and beliefs. This will then lead us, as teachers and educators, to examine our own contribution to and, in fact, support of some of the oppressive structures present in schools. It is imperative then that we begin first to understand with other teachers our knowledge positions; then we can critically engage and value student and parent voices as part of the continuing dialogue, giving them value as knowledgeable human beings who also function in the creation of knowledge and meaning in the world.

Freire (1998) asserts that we must respect the knowledge that students carry with them by engaging students in dialogue around questions such as:

1. What are the concrete realities of their lives and the aggressive reality in which violence is permanent and where people are more familiar with death than with life?
2. What are the intimate connections between knowledge considered basic to any school curriculum and knowledge that is the fruit of the lived experience of students as individuals?
3. What are the implications, political and ideological, of the neglect of the poor areas of the city by the constituted authorities? Are there class-related ethical questions that need to be looked at here? (pp. 36–37).

It is probably clear at this point that it is my belief that we also engage the above questions as part of reflecting on our own lived realities and experiences. You may agree that this work needs to be engaged by all teachers, but argue that such critical reflection is rarely found as part of teacher professional development. This occurs because most school districts, while committed to teacher growth and development, usually view teachers as technicians who are to be developed by giving them more techniques rather than asking them to engage in critical dialogue. Cochran-Smith and Lytle (1993) state that "in many school systems … teachers have not been encouraged to work together on voluntary, self-initiated projects or to speak out with authority about instructional, curricular, and policy issues" (p. 21). Such critical and dialogical processes between and among teachers in schools requires administrators in schools and districts to acknowledge the talent and professionalism of teachers. In doing so they cannot just say, "we want collaboration," but must consciously provide spaces and time that allow for true collaborative, democratic processes. Thus, by enacting the principle of historicity of knowledge all teachers can begin to be participants in their own learning. In doing so they can unveil the hegemony of the literacy and other school curricula, and function as more critical educators both with students and peers alike.

While I may be idealistic, I am also realistic and recognize that in order to have schools that are transformative, that value teachers as professionals and intellectuals rather than technicians in need of development, schools need to place less emphasis on goals and processes related to socialization—that "imitation, participation, and obedience to instruction and command"—and place great emphasis on educational processes, such as "two-way communication, initiative, creativity, and criticism." By doing so the outcomes, or truths, rather than being the "acquisition of habits, skills and attitudes," would be "the acquisition of attitudes and dispositions, knowledge and skills that are individualized and critically thoughtful" (Arnstine, 1995, p. 10).

So while many schools may have as their mission, and rightly so, to socialize students into our democratic society and world, those responsible for educating children need to ensure through critical inquiry that one process does not dominate over the other. To achieve this balance requires that each of us involved in schools reflect critically on our values, beliefs, and truths, and be open to reflection and dialogue with others, including our students and their parents. Further, we must do this while understanding that there is no absolute truth, but multiple truths, understanding that truths are derived first and foremost from our own lived realities, experiences, and histories. The challenge for us as educators and as a society is to be open to this dialectic and embrace and learn from the complexities and chaos of such varying ideas and ideals (Freire, 1993).

Part II:
Linking Literacy Ideology & Policy to Teacher Practice

While Part I linked the ideology and forms of literacy with public policy for literacy and bilingual instruction, as well as the elements of critical theory, Part II of this text connects instructional approaches and the curriculum related to literacy learning and development to ideology and public policy. It is this next level, curriculum and instruction, that must be examined in order to fully engage our own beliefs about literacy and the resulting teaching-learning processes. The following chapters are concerned first with the pedagogical approaches, programs, and institutional practices found in schools. Examples from teacher practice will be shared to highlight the educational processes reflective of the public policies of oral, signature, recitation, and decoding/analyzing literacies and their ideological connections and effects on teachers and students in classroom contexts. That is, how programmed literacy orientations are reflected in teaching methods, curricula evaluation, and student interaction. The goal is to begin to uncover the hidden curriculum within the approaches and programming for literacy and language development presently part of ELD, SDAIE content classes, structured English immersion, and mainstream English classes for remedial skills development.

Chapter 4
Engaging Literacy Ideology & Pedagogy

Language minority students have been invisible and silent in all too many classrooms across our nation, from underrepresentation in textbooks to the persistent policies and practices that consider the use of languages other than English to be a serious handicap or deficit. Results of this invisibility and silence are depressingly familiar: inordinately high dropout rates, diminished self-esteem, and disproportionately high rates of failure in general in our public schools (Nieto, 1996, p. 147).

When considering the teaching of English to students of other languages it is important to consider the literacy of their home and culture as well as the underlying values and assumptions inherent in our own practices. Myers (1996) and others (Brice-Heath, 1983; Street, 1984; Gee, 1990) point out that different selves can be found in the different forms of literacy. Here, each form of public policy literacy is revisited briefly to link it to instructional practices found in second-language classrooms (ELD) and content-area classrooms (SDAIE) where instruction is conducted in English. The connections of each to ideology and bilingual education are illustrated in Table 1, Framework for Engaging Literacy Ideology Policy & Practice, found in Chapter 2, p. 19. It should be noted that the methods and processes highlighted in Table 1 are those most prevalent in schools presently, and that other forms of engagement are possible. Only those articulated in recent research literature deemed as best practices are reviewed here, because it is these practices that are most commonly represented in the research literature and in classrooms.

As I have advocated in this text, researchers, teachers, and educators must begin to recognize the political ideologies related to the literacy curriculum, and then be prepared to acknowledge that all students bring with them not only language and culture, but different forms of literacy. To begin this process, the following analysis of literacy forms and their connection to practice attempts to demonstrate that literacy forms, which are valued and promoted in schools, may not adequately reflect the form of literacy familiar to or valued within the language, culture, community, or homes of many students. As a result of my own teaching experiences and research in schools, these examples of student engagement are detailed to demonstrate that when teachers promote and, further, value one form of literacy over another, they are at the same time devaluing and possibly dehumanizing students who may not accept or understand the legitimate form of literacy that is part of the curriculum and teaching methods most commonly promoted and utilized by state-adopted texts and resulting programs (Brice-Heath, 1983; Bartolome, 1994; Macedo, 1994; Myers, 1996).

As will be demonstrated, while many strategies (i.e., cooperative learning, reciprocal teaching, and whole language) may have the *potential* to transform students into active subjects and participants in their own learning, it is only potential because, as Bartolome (1994) emphasizes, "the most pedagogically sound strategy can be rendered useless by teachers who do not master their areas of specialization and / or who do not view their students as capable learners who bring valuable life experience and language skills to the classroom" (p. 211). It is crucial to this review to understand that each approach is engaged based on its theoretical definition, with examples of implementation that may or may not reflect the intent of the underlying theory, but of the adapted practice or teachers' interpretation of that practice.

Oral Literacy

As stated in Chapter 2, oral approaches to literacy value the individual and community literacy over institutional literacies. That is, "normal children throughout the world acquire their maternal oral language(s) relatively easily at a similar rate regardless of the language," where oral language is a required feature of all material and human circumstances (Macias, 1989, p. 19). Hence, oral forms of literacy value orality over the written word. Through orality individuals interpret and apply language in given social interactions and situations. Oral literacy, more often than not, is acquired rather than learned. Gee (1990) clarifies the difference between acquisition and learning:

Acquisition is a process of acquiring something subconsciously by exposure to models, a process of trial and error, and practice within social groups, without formal teaching. It happens in natural settings which are meaningful and functional in the sense that acquirers know that they need to acquire the thing they are exposed to in order to function and that they in fact want to so function. This is how most people come to control their first language.

Learning is a process that involves conscious knowledge gained through teaching (though not necessarily from someone officially designated a teacher) or through certain life-experiences that trigger conscious reflection. This teaching or reflection involves explanation and analysis, that is, breaking down the thing to be learned into is analytic parts. It inherently involves attaining, along with the matter being taught, some degree of meta-knowledge about the matter (p. 146).

This distinction is important to consider when linking forms of literacy to educational practice. When articulating approaches of teaching for ELLs, it has been recognized that language is best learned in an environment that fosters acquisition as part of the learning process (Krashen & Terrell, 1983). For example, an acquisition lesson would have its focus on vocabulary and situations that are reflective of the life of the community in which the students live and have a need to function, rather than on isolated vocabulary or grammar that is not contextualized within a real-life setting (Krashen & Terrell, 1983).

An oral orientation toward literacy is reflected in ESL classrooms where students dictate stories using the Language Experience Approach (Richard-Amato, 1996). In this approach to language learning, student voice and story form the basis of the written content. As such, a higher value is placed on oral expression because the text is created by students individually or in groups and then read. Such a form of literacy is part of a student-centered approach not typically supported by conservative policy makers or educational administrators because it encourages the use of teacher- and student-created content over published texts (Shannon, 1989; Macedo, 1994; Myers, 1996). Content and text is further derived from authentic sources including news reports, newspapers, and other oral and written discourses. One example of this comes from my own teaching experience:

Students in my beginning-level ESL class created a written text from oral discussions around a trip they took to the zoo. It began when I asked students to retell one experience each; from these I created a narrative that became a model for their own narrative pieces.

Such an oral form of literacy can be extended further to engage students in critical dialogue around social issues of language, race, class, and gender. In Mr. Clark's high school beginning-level ESL classroom I observed the following:

> Mr. Clark asked students to tell stories of individuals who impacted their lives (i.e., relatives, friends, immediate family) and then asked the students to talk in pairs and list characteristics of these individuals. When they were finished they compared the descriptions of those familiar to them to the characteristics of historical figures (i.e., Martin Luther King Jr., Cesar Chavez, Harriet Tubman, etc.) they were researching.

In both my classroom and the one observed, students' language errors were not corrected; that is, the intent was to get students to utilize oral language to express their understanding and observations. It was not focused on correct usage or form, but on encouraging communication to convey ideas, concepts, and beliefs, which is reflective of the communicative approach to language development (Krashen, 1994). Further, both experiences facilitated processes of vocabulary development.

Based on these examples, it could be supposed that oral literacy is an early form of a critical literacy approach. However, due to its organic nature and potential for social empowerment, oral literacy has not been determined a legitimate form of literacy, which is one reason it has not resurfaced as a public policy literacy since the 18th century (Shannon, 1989; Myers, 1996). The historical development of print literacy, in many respects reflects the natural approach to writing acquisition (Krashen, 1994) and whole-language approaches (Edelsky, Altwerger, & Flores, 1991) that most language teachers are familiar with.

As can be seen, oral and communicative processes are centered on student voice where their contributions are valued as part of the language learning process not separate from it. Ideologically, these approaches to oral literacy are mostly progressive in nature and have the potential to engage a critical ideology as well. These connections to ideology are reflected in the framework depicted in Table 1 on page 19 which further connects oral literacy to a more permissive and quality model of bilingual education.

Signature Literacy

From a historical educational perspective, signature literacy places the student self as a passive, silent, mental muscle sitting at a desk bolted to the floor, engaging in mental exercises like copying, while waiting for the teacher to provide the advice of a moral police-person (Myers, 1996). Signature literacy is reflected in modern classroom practices where students copy words from the board, definitions from dictionaries, and predetermined vocabulary lists for content area instruction. Such activities take place in many high school English classrooms where teachers are focused on developing vocabulary and correct word usage (Myers, 1996). In one of the high school ESL classrooms I observed the following:

> The teacher, Mrs. Garcia, gave the class a dictionary exercise where she had 15 words on the overhead. She directed students to individually copy the words and look them up in the dictionary and write one definition. While all of the students followed the directions, about half did not understand the words they were looking up, they didn't know which definition to write, and many had to wait for the teacher to guide them to the correct definition.

While this example illustrates a very common practice for introducing students to new words, research has indicated that it does little to increase a student's vocabulary or spelling abilities (Lapp & Flood, 1983; Krashen, 1993; Cox, 1999). When students copy words and definitions they do not utilize oral language to negotiate meaning, and most often such activities are completed independently, which further limits language development and student voice (Krashen, 1993; Richard-Amato, 1996).

In addition, signature literacy practices seem to be most effective for language development when they are linked to a real-world context and reflect communicative approaches that allow students to bring meaning to text and vocabulary (Krashen & Terrell, 1983; Cummins, 1989). Such progressive literacy orientations can be seen when children attempt to write their names, create symbols to represent words and thoughts, and use inventive spelling to convey oral concepts via print (Krashen & Terrell, 1983; Edelsky, Altwerger, & Flores, 1991). As part of the same unit from Mr. Clark's ESL classroom I observed the following vocabulary exercise:

> Mr. Clark was introducing the word "struggle"—a word that the students needed to incorporate into biographies they were researching and writing on famous heroes (i.e., Cesar Chavez, Sojourner Truth, Gandhi). When Mr. Clark asked students to share what they thought the word meant, no one responded. Realizing the students did not understand the new word, Mr. Clark walked to

the blackboard and drew a figure (Figure 2). It was drawing of a man pushing a box, with one box on the incline and another on a flat surface.

Figure 2: Methaphor for Struggle

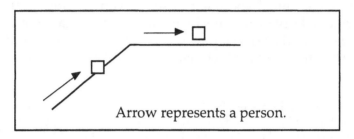

Arrow represents a person.

Once the drawing was complete and he asked students, "What is easier, pushing the box up the hill [points to the incline] or pushing a box across a floor [points to flat surface]?" He also acted out each movement physically. Once students began to respond that pushing the box up the hill would be harder, heavier, more difficult than pushing it across the floor, he put the word struggle under the incline. Mr. Clark then called on students individually and asked each student to read a portion of their biography. After each student read from their story, he asked him or her, "At this point in your story is the person going up [points to the arrow at the bottom of Figure 2] or are they at the top [refers to top arrow in Figure 2]?" After students answered, he asked them to identify passages in their stories where the word struggle might be appropriately used.

The use of metaphor and physical acting out in this activity was very powerful, and although there was some confusion in the beginning and it took some time to process what the teacher was getting at, the students really understood the concept of struggle. They also learned other vocabulary words as more students read from their biographies and described what they believed were struggles their leaders encountered. Also modeled here was the use of dialogue in debating whether the examples students shared were actually struggles or more appropriately obstacles or problems.

As in oral literacy, the examples here illustrate the benefits when teachers recognize that use of a particular form of literacy can make a difference, has value, and then can be considered legitimate. As reflected here and in Table 1, signature literacy can be both ideologically functional and progressive, but it depends on the teaching approach that is taken. It is important to note that I do believe it is absolutely necessary for students to learn dictionary usage, conventions of spelling, handwriting, and vocabulary development; however, I believe the process that brings students to this learned understanding has the potential to be either empowering or disempowering (Bartolome, 1994; Macedo, 1994). As a result it becomes important to reflect both on the fundamentals we teach and the processes we utilize in teaching these necessary and fundamental literacy skills.

Recitation Literacy

Recitation literacy views the student self as an empty vessel into which the teacher, sitting on a raised platform and playing the role of information authority, pours knowledge into the student (Myers, 1996). In such an environment, students memorize dialogues and prepared scripts. This is common in the audio-lingual method of second-language instruction where students are required to learn and memorize scripted dialogues and perform or recite them back (Richard-Amato, 1996; Richards & Rogers, 1997).

For example, in many ESL materials for beginning speakers you can find short dialogues in books or on tapes. In some classrooms teachers will have students recite and memorize the dialogue word for word, and repeat them several times with the intent of developing fluency and pronunciation. However, such methods can negate student voice and intellect and further treat the student as an entity separate from the discourse of power and transformation (Kelly, 1997). This is reflected in what Freire (1993) refers to as the "banking model" of teaching, "where the teacher issues communiqués and makes deposits which the students patiently receive, memorize, and repeat" (p. 53). Recitation literacy is also mirrored in a cultural ideology where in many classrooms across our country, students are required to recite certain passages, like the Gettysburg Address or the preamble to the U.S. Constitution.

These documents are identified by Hirsch (1988) as part of cultural knowledge that is necessary for every American child to know in order to be a literate citizen. It is imperative from a critical perspective that we question not only the processes but the content of such activities (Macedo, 1994). Reading, memorizing, and automatically repeating historical facts or passages doesn't lead students to question or engage how or why we come to know and recite certain passages; that is, do students really understand why they are required to memorize and recite the Gettysburg Address? Because recitation literacy is focused primarily on oral production in a formal manner, it is only necessary to know where the document originates historically. In its historical time period, students who were taught through recitation had to memorize and recite biblical verse (Myers, 1996). This form of literacy is inherently connected to cultural ideologies, but can be engaged in a more progressive manner. For example, if students are given the opportunity to create dialogue, explore other cultural texts, and re-present those ideas in a formal oral presentation, then recitation occurs, but with a more critical engagement of the material. This form of cultural literacy can be linked to more progressive teaching methods such as a whole-language approach for reading or communicative approach for English-language development. It is within the latter that students create dialogues to inform linguistic structures (i.e., debate, argumentation) as well as develop academic language skills (Krashen, 1994).

Students in one of the classrooms I observed participated in the following recitation activity through a communicative process:

> The teacher, Mrs. Rodriguez, distributed to students in groups of three a dialogue between a waiter and two patrons in a restaurant. The teacher first read the dialogue. The students then repeated, in unison, the reading of the dialogue focusing on pronunciation and word order. Students then read the dialogue in groups two or three times with Mrs. Rodriguez going to each group and providing models, correction, and feedback. After they were comfortable with the script, Mrs. Rodriguez asked each group of students to create their own dialogue in a restaurant or other place where two friends might go after school (i.e., music store, grocery store, etc.). Before starting, students contributed ideas and vocabulary that Mrs. Rodriguez wrote on the board. She then construed a model dialogue that she left on the overhead for student reference. Students worked for the remainder of the class period on their dialogues. For homework they were required to practice and memorize their dialogues to perform in front of the class the following day.

In this activity, the students had the opportunity to build fluency and practice pronunciation from both a textbook-constructed text and a self-constructed text. In addition, they were required to memorize a dialogue, as this was necessary for completing the final assignment. However, the final text was generated from a model where students could add language and their own voice to the piece. Recitation was utilized, but as in the previous forms of literacy, it is necessary to reflect on both the content of the curriculum and the process utilized to achieve linguistic outcomes for student success.

Another element in recitation literacy is that of lecture. It is important to note that teacher lecture is not something that one should *not* do in a classroom; on the contrary, there are times when it is necessary and efficient. When observing Mrs. Rodriguez teach this lesson, she went to and from group work to whole class instruction several times in order to ensure students understood the assignment. The following example illustrates what happens when clear direct instruction is not provided to students:

> In Mrs. Garcia's beginning-level ESL class the assignment was for students to write a news report based on a story of a car accident they had read about. From the front of the class Mrs. Garcia called on individual students to take turns reading the story, in a round-robin style. As soon as the reading was finished, she assigned the students to groups and gave each a specific role as a news reporter: one student was a reporter at the news station, another was the reporter on the scene, and a third was a reporter at the hospital. All of the instructions were given orally. As Mrs. Garcia explained the assignment, students were in their assigned groups, some were talking, and most were not sure what they were supposed to do. This assignment, while well intentioned, caused much confusion. The students only had the story text in front of them, and they were not provided with any scaffolds or written models to base this task on. As a result, they didn't understand all of the language or how to take the text of the story, which was in narrative form, and convert it to the language of a news report. The goal was to have students present in the next class session, but for two more class sessions I observed Mrs. Garcia go around to different groups explaining and reexplaining what she wanted them to write, read, and perform. When they did finally present their dialogues two days later, they had to read them from the scripts because they had no time to rehearse.

While this lesson was creative in that students were able to construct dialogue, it was also problematic because the directions were not clearly stated and even the goals of the lesson were not clear to either me, the observer, or the students—that is, was the goal oral production or to understand the various roles of news reporters? From the above examples it is clear that recitation literacy can be a useful technique in involving students in authentic processes to facilitate learning and oral production of key syntax, oral fluency, and vocabulary. However, without a clear understanding of the purpose of the task or its relevance it may do little to promote literacy and language development to a critical or personal level. As reflected in Table 1, recitation literacy, while most closely tied to a cultural ideology, can also be progressive and critical if engaged in critically by either analyzing the text to be recited or providing a model for an authentic text to be created. As for teacher-centeredness, it is clear that teacher direction is a critical element in conveying the complexity and goals of the end performance this literacy requires.

Decoding/Analytic

Reading does not consist merely of decoding the written word or language; rather it is preceded by and intertwined with knowledge of the word. Language and reality are dynamically interconnected. The understanding attained by critical reading of a text implies perceiving the relationship between text and context (Freire, 1993, p. 29).

In the early 20th century the decoding, analytic approach to literacy viewed the student as a factory worker who needed to have his/her schoolwork managed, segmented, and organized around prefabricated assembly lines of intellectual work and text (Myers, 1996). In actuality, this form of literacy was not a form that was part of a linguistic community or group, but rather an imposed literacy, and the question of what we learn to read became

inextricably bound up with the question of how one learns to read. Unfortunately, experience shows that the methods which most readily and efficiently bring about skills to read (or write, or figure) in its narrower sense of ability to recognize, pronounce and put together words, do not at the same time take care of the formation of attitudes that decide the uses to which the ability is to be put (Dewey, 1959, p. 110).

Different from the oral and signature traditions that came from the community, a functional methodology or solely a banking approach toward literacy and reading instruction is inarguably efficient, but has long been known not to allow for the development of social and critical thought (Dewey, 1959; Freire, 1993).

The analytic or decoding form of literacy, based on the scientific approach, is most often seen in the phonics method, where students are taught sound-symbol relationships, combinations of symbols, and the rules governing their use (Adams, 1990). Within an ELD classroom, this didactic approach to teaching literacy is often seen in a grammar curriculum, where teachers focus on the instruction of grammar rules, grammar and vocabulary drills, and the teaching of reading comprehension as a systematic method (Shannon, 1989), or in the process of teaching phonemic awareness, a skill that has been scientifically shown to be a necessary precursor to the ability to read (Yopp, 1992). In the ELD classroom the teacher who uses a grammar approach usually has curriculum materials that are designed for specific levels of language learners, with graded readers and activities that are reductionistic in nature (Macedo, 1994).

The "exclusive use of structural approaches to teaching reading and writing, which are for the most part phonics- and grammar-based, fail to meet the needs of second language students with low-literacy backgrounds" (Hamayan, 1994, p. 288). This is not to imply that the teaching of functional literacy isn't important or necessary, but that when the approach is taken in a purely technical form that doesn't engage student experience or voice, it has the potential to limit not only language development but participation in society (Brice-Heath, 1983; Edelsky, Altwerger, & Flores, 1991; Brisk & Harrington, 2000).

> During the 2001–2002 school year I had the opportunity to visit eight junior and senior high schools in a local school district. In the junior high schools I visited, I made a point to visit the basic-skills English and reading classes. In many of these classrooms, students were grouped according to reading ability, with no more than 20 to 25 students per class. In these classrooms students worked from the basal texts, which included graded reading passages and stories. In most of the classrooms I visited, after students spent from 15 to 30 minutes reading a common text out loud, either in whole class or small groups, they then completed workbook assignments. Most often this part of the class took from 20 to 30 minutes; students worked independently or in pairs completing spelling, vocabulary, grammar, or comprehension exercises. Students interacted very little with each other, and creative writing occurred in journal writing and reading response logs. For the most part, the teacher controlled instruction, and students moved in unison through assignments and activities.

The teachers in the classrooms I visited all felt that students were progressing very well and were catching up with grade-level peers. I agree with these teachers—there was little doubt that these students were learning to read and making progress in that they were becoming successful in learning how to decode instructional-level text and demonstrate comprehension of text through multiple-choice and short-answer exercises. However, some teachers were concerned that the curriculum failed to engage students in deeper critical thinking activities or utilize literature that was relevant to their language, culture, or community lives. I strongly agree with Harman and Edelsky (1989) that "merely knowing how to read and write guarantees neither membership in the dominant culture nor the concomitant political, economic, cognitive, or social rewards of that membership" (p. 393). So, ideologically, an analytic/decoding literacy is most often functional in nature, and as Table 1 indicates, this form of literacy tends to predominate over the course of time and is also linked with more restrictive forms of bilingual education. Thus, as was stated with oral, signature, and recitation literacies, the form of literacy and its resulting curricula and teaching methods cannot be ignored, but need to be engaged mindfully by examining how they address culture, language, and student voice.

So, if all of these forms of literacy have elements in our curricula, but none are sufficient in and of themselves, then how is a teacher to proceed? How do curriculum developers, administrators, and teachers decide what is important? That is, if students are reading below grade level, isn't it more important to teach them the skills as quickly as possible using basal and direct instruction programs? Isn't it also appropriate to use the most efficient method to get students to read and then worry about being creative later? These are comments that most teachers have and they are valid, but if we want to educate students to be advocates for themselves, to be critical thinkers and writers as well as having the ability to speak and read with initiative and creativity, then how do we proceed? I suggest, and Myers' (1996) work supports, a notion for a new standard of literacy. Within this new standard approach, no one method is validated as being better than another; rather all methods and approaches are valued as being equally important and necessary. This new standard also necessitates promoting an awareness of the sociopolitical contexts in which such curricula are developed and intentioned. It is toward such a standard we now turn.

New Standard Approaches

It was neither text nor instructional processes that led to the mastery of standard English communication skills, but the nature of teachers' beliefs regarding their prior educational experience and the nature of their current relationships with children (Hollingsworth & Gallego, 1996, p. 271).

Knowledge within a new standard of literacy is embodied in the beliefs and pedagogies of teachers, and the actions and lives of students. These realities can be found in both student-created text and authentic literature. Text, within this standard, includes instructional and authentic materials that engage, illustrate, and encourage culturally diverse views. In such a classroom, students select reading materials, create text, and engage in active dialogue and deconstruction of texts and their meanings. These processes are facilitated by teachers in ESL and SDAIE classrooms who use the Natural Approach (Krashen &

Terrell, 1983) to language development. Teachers begin this engagement by placing the students' lives and language skills at the center of instruction (Krashen, 1994; Richard-Amato, 1996). In this classroom a student's first language is valued and can be used to negotiate meaning. Such an environment supports language development while using real-life, personal, and social issues to encourage conversation and dialogue. Within ELD and SDAIE classrooms, an approach such as this encompasses all the language skills, including listening, speaking, reading, and writing. Collier (1987) states: "Language is the focus of every content-area task, with all meaning and all demonstration of knowledge expressed through oral and written forms of language" (p. 618). These approaches toward literacy are meant to engage both monolingual and bilingual students because literacy development in any language should involve all the same skills and processes that make students' language and culture a core element in the curriculum.

I will conclude with the following classroom observation. This observation and the resulting conversation with Mrs. Rodriguez begin to reveal several ideologies of literacy than can function within one lesson.

Mrs. Rodriquez began class by asking students to write a journal about their parents' jobs. This journal prompt came from the *Grammar in Action* text. The text suggested using this activity as a scaffold to the lesson on how to construct question formations and use prepositions. After the students finished writing, several read their journals to the class; then Mrs. Rodriguez asked students to call out the professions they had written about. The list on the overhead was laid out as follows:

painter (paints houses)	painter (paints cars)
car salesman	fisherman (goes out in fishing boats)
body shop worker	auto mechanic
janitor	boss
maintenance worker	construction worker

After the students completed this list, Mrs. Rodriguez introduced the grammar lesson, which included the following list of professions: real estate agent, accountant, lawyer, doctor. In order for the students to understand the exercise Mr. Rodriguez had to define the professions, since these words were new to most of the students. After introducing the word list, the bell rang for a nutrition break. During the break I asked Mrs. Rodriguez to look at the list of professions the students generated on the board and compare them to those in the text. She immediately stated that "trades describe the types of jobs the students related and 'professions' reflected those in the text." She reflected at that moment that she had done this exercise many times and never made a connection between the list generated by the students and the list in the text. She stated "I just use this journal prompt as a way to get them thinking about jobs, I never really considered the types of jobs." When the students returned from break she lead a discussion about the differences between trades and professions. She attempted to give value to the students and their parents' jobs by saying that all are important contributors to the functioning of society.

Although Mrs. Rodriguez continued the lesson in the text by instructing students to use the professions listed, I felt she could have pushed further and allowed students to complete the same grammar activity using the professions of their parents and family members along with those in the book, which they could not relate to. In order to meet a new standard and engage both instructional content and incorporate more progressive and critical ideologies, this lesson could include the following addition. After the activity, where students have used both the text-suggested professions and the ones they generated on the board, the following questions could be posed for student discussion:

1. Why do you think your parents don't have these jobs we see in the book?
2. Who do you think has these jobs? Why? Who wrote the book? What perspective is this book written from?
3. What skills or knowledge is required to be a lawyer, doctor, etc.? Why?
4. What skills or knowledge are required to be a carpenter?
5. Which professions are valued more in our society? In the country you come from? Why?
6. Do you they think it is fair that some jobs are valued differently than others?

Mrs. Rodriguez did include some of these questions the following day, and encouraged students to interview their parents and family members regarding their training, knowledge, and skills. In this manner the curriculum, which was static in the text, came alive and began to take into account both the teacher and student perspective. Additionally, they used English to not only learn the grammar lesson, but to analyze the social and political issues related to equity, fairness, and justice.

Reflective Activity: Think of a reading, literacy, or other language-based lesson you have taught recently and write a brief response to the following questions:

1) How many of the different literacies discussed here are exemplified in your lesson or activity?

2) What ideologies are represented?

3) How do you communicate literacy via the lesson? As a decoding/analytic process or some other process?

4) Based on this reading, what would you change, modify, add, or take away from the lesson or activity? Why? What results would you expect or anticipate?

5) Discuss your reflection and lesson activity/lesson with a colleague. What is his/her opinion and/or viewpoint?

Chapter 5
Institutional Practices &
Effects of Literacy Ideologies

The majority of teachers, consciously or unconsciously, reproduce a variety of authoritarian practices related to classroom management in their efforts to maintain "control" of their students. On the other hand, teachers who struggle to implement more liberating strategies, often are forced to become masters of deception—saying what the principal or district office wishes to hear, while doing behind closed doors what they truly believe is in concert with an emancipatory vision of education (Darder, 2002, p. 97).

This chapter reflects on two different approaches to school and classroom practices utilized to develop literacy in secondary settings. The first illustration, focusing on tracking and ability grouping, summarizes the literature related to this common conservative approach to teaching students from marginalized groups. Programs that reflect tracking are currently on the rise as schools move toward strict accountability measures in response to the federal No Child Left Behind Act. These skill-based programs are often promoted as the *only* way to teach students who are underprepared (Oakes, 1985; Auerbach, 1991; Apple, 1995), and that without these basic skills students will be at risk of not being successful in American society. This practice is connected with the policies of functional and cultural literacies previously discussed and defined in Chapter 1.

The second illustration is that of critical literacy classroom practices that promote students as participants in their own literacy development. The goal of this approach is to empower students. This is accomplished by providing students with critical-thinking and problem-posing strategies and techniques that teach them to become active participants in a democratic society. This approach is characteristic of the progressive and critical ideologies discussed in Chapter 2 of this text.

The purpose of these critical illustrations is to provide a context within which teachers can reflect further on their own practice and the policy and practices in their schools. These two different approaches not only exist within schools and classrooms, but also come into conflict when teachers are attempting to function within the political context of schools. Very often we as teachers consciously or unconsciously reproduce a variety of teaching practices and methods, but only within a critical perspective are the more common unconscious actions engaged or revealed (Darder, 2002). As the literature in Part I illustrates, "common practices come not from divining decree, but from choices made sometime, somewhere" (Hinchey, 1998, p. 7). However, most teachers remain unaware of how the text and processes they use may not serve to reach the goals they so desire (Apple, 1986). To this end, this final examination provides a lens through which to view the present practice of the four ideological positions that have been the focus of this book. This chapter reveals the final movement from theory to practice, and highlights the dichotomies and tensions of the process that I engaged in my own practice as a classroom teacher, as a researcher working with teachers, and as a teacher educator.

Tracking and Ability Grouping

What diminishes human rationality is the thwarting of flexible human intelligence by prescriptions that shackle the educational imagination (Eisner, 1994, p. 165).

In order to understand the institutional impact of most literacy and English curricula and instruction on students in junior and senior high schools, it is best to begin by examining how policy makers and educators understand the word *curriculum*. I argue that it is, in part, the misguided, or politically intended interpretation of this word that provides the rationale for policies such as institutional tracking, common curriculum for varying levels of learners, overrepresentation of certain ethnic and socioeconomic groups in advanced placement and remedial classes, and justification for varying teaching methods according to perceived group ability or inability.

Joe Kincheloe (1998), in his article, "Pinar's Currere and Identity in Hyperreality: Grounding the Post-formal Notion of Intrapersonal Intelligence," relates an important concept about how we interpret curriculum in terms of the history of the word itself. The noun *curriculum* is derived from the Latin verb *currere*, which means "running a race course, an action." However, in education, the present (and much of the past) interpretation of the word is reduced to the noun form, which means "the track." This difference in definition is crucial for it implies that curriculum, as it is commonly used, is dictated and static, not fluid or changing.

> Mainstream educators forget that curriculum is an active process; it is not sim-
> ply the lesson plan, the district guidebook, the standardized test, the goals and
> milestones, or the textbook. The curriculum, Slattery continues, is a holistic
> life experience, the journey of becoming a self-aware subject capable of shap-
> ing his or her life path (Slattery in Kincheloe, 1998, p. 129).

When this interpretation is applied to the literacy curriculum in schools, it is far too easy to see how the noun form has flourished when we look at the instructional practice of tracking or ability grouping. This occurs in the English curriculum when students are grouped according to their reading levels, thus dictating which curriculum they will receive. Within this approach there is no journey or exploration of self or other, but rather a well-worn track that is constricted with checkpoints, limits, and a defined end. Additionally, and most importantly, such skill-based groupings are forms of social control that function to "provide differential forms of schooling to different classes of students" (Giroux, 1983, p. 47).

Much research has been completed in examining tracking or skill grouping practices in schools in relation to teacher perceptions and student outcomes. In a study on tracking practices in junior and senior high schools, Oakes (1985) found that most educators felt groups of similar students were easier to teach. These same educators also held the belief that students learned better in groups that included others like themselves. Further, teachers modified their practice and curriculum to their expectations of student achievement, based on test scores and perceived outcomes. The problematic condition here is that well-intentioned educators are unaware of their role in perpetuating social stratification and believe that by maintaining the status quo they are serving their students appropriately (Giroux, 1983; Apple, 1986).

A further indicator of social stratification is the lack of diversity represented in such ability groupings. Oakes (1985) and Olsen (1997) found that there exists a noticeable lack of ethnic diversity in classrooms where students are grouped according to ability. They relate that those students in higher tracks are more likely to be children of parents who have gone to college and are white. Oakes (1985) reported that in a school where 46% to 53% of the population was white, an average of 62% of the students in the high-track English courses were white, versus the low-track classes, where 29% were white. These statistics were also mirrored in the junior and senior high schools I visited in 2001 and 2002. Further, in both my observations and Olsen's (1997) study of a school where "no single ethnic group constitutes a majority and a common home language does not span more than half of the student body" (p. 36), the lower track or skills courses were disproportionately Latino and black, while the college prep classes were disproportionately Asian and white. It is also imperative to note that "this racial reality is not commented on, noticed, or acknowledged by most teachers" (Olsen, 1997, p. 188). This fact is revealing in that it reflects the strong hegemonic filter that is pervasive to the point that teachers truly believe that it is a students' merit that dictates his/her ability to achieve, not considering that it can be otherwise. As a result, the differences found in the lower and higher tracks also reflect class differences, where students in the higher tracks are from higher socioeconomic backgrounds. Such devastating overrepresentations and distinctions are not acknowledged and are rarely addressed as areas of concern by many educators (Olsen, 1997; Oakes, 1985). Oakes (1985) reports that "teachers sometimes mention issues of culture when describing students in the top or lower tracks of school, but the implications or specifics behind such references are not mentioned" (p. 188). Overall, teachers believe that all students can "make it" or be in honors classes if they are willing to apply themselves and work hard to get good grades, or make it out of remedial classes. Here the responsibility for achievement rests solely with the student because the system is providing the curriculum and scientifically based teaching methods. In the research conducted by Olsen (1997), teachers' statements reveal their strong belief in meritocracy: "Students who are in the skills classes, are the ones who don't care about school, don't care about their future, don't try" (p. 188).

In the end, the variety of curricula used by schools reflects the expectations that the larger society and educators hold for certain groups of students (Apple, 1979). For example, when a group of students is seen as being composed of prospective members of a professional and managerial class (high track), then the literacy curriculum is more likely to be organized around flexibility, choice, and inquiry. However, students who are seen as being prospective members of a working or skill class are provided with a curriculum that stresses punctuality, neatness, habit formation, and vocational skills that reflect an education for socialization (Arnstine, 1995). Such views, however, are not often recognized by teachers. This is true most often because we haven't had the opportunity, or been encouraged in our institutions, to critically examine the historical relationship and deep ties education has, and continues to maintain, to the economic, political, and cultural conflicts that are part of this country (Apple, 1986; Darder, 1991; Apple, 1995; Giroux, 1996). Further, teachers too often "place educational questions in a separate compartment, one that does not easily allow for interaction with the relations of class, gender, and racial power that give education its social meaning" (Apple, 1986, p. 5).

In light of the above, it is imperative that teachers and educators begin to critically analyze these oppressive practices, which not only still exist, but are becoming more prevalent in schools across the country as policies such as No Child Left Behind make explicit the rhetoric of scientific research, and take a one-size-fits-all approach to teaching and literacy development. As I hope you have found through your own reflections in the reading of this book, a critical analysis allows for a deeper understanding of the political structures that support oppressive practices which are impacted by racist, sexist, linguistic, and class-biased notions of human potential (Bowles & Gintes, 1971; Giroux, 1983; Darder, 1991; Levine, 1995). We, as teachers and educators, owe it to our students and society to acknowledge that practices such as ability testing and tracking are a form of social control and a systematic way of sorting children along ethnic, racial, class, and gender lines. The consequences of such activities are devastating to far too many of our young people and the political forces that sustain such efforts must be critically examined and dismantled (Giroux, 1983).

One of the teachers I worked with in my research felt frustrated by the high number of students in his 11th grade U.S. history class who were identified as low performers. That is, the majority of the total of 37 students were Latino, bilingual, and no longer receiving ELD instruction, even though most had reading levels far below grade level. He was encouraged by his administrators to use SDAIE strategies to teach the content.

Mr. Delgado's classroom is set up in traditional rows, with the teacher's desk in the back of the room and podium in the front. The room is very crowded with little room for movement between rows. On the days that I observe there are usually between 33 and 37 students in attendance. The students are pre-pared for class, they know the routine and are respectful toward the teacher and each other by listening and following directions. Every day he teaches the class from the front of the room, standing at the podium. He has an agenda on the board and usually starts the class by having individual students read por-tions of the text or questions from the board. Mr. Delgado has a very positive rapport with the students. He values individual student responses and has a great ability to validate all responses (answers to questions of content) even when the answers he receives are not the ones he is expecting or looking for. This is truly a gift, as Mr. Delgado can take an answer that is far from what he wants and make it relevant. For example, one day when discussing the Civil War, a student responded with a fact that was about the American Revolution. Rather than indicating it wasn't correct, Mr. Delgado made a connection be-tween the past war and the one they were discussing. I observed him do this many times throughout my visits. In addition, he critically presents concepts related to democracy and freedom that students should think about as related to their own lives, and he poses real critical reflection questions around issues of race, class, and gender. Despite these positive approaches on Mr. Delgado's part, the majority of the students don't respond. They sit quietly and passively during most reading and lectures. Further, all written assignments were to be completed individually, even though many students had difficulty reading and writing.

While this is a very caring teacher who has expertise and a critical aware-ness of this content area, he felt he wasn't succeeding in teaching his students and wanted to consider what he could do to better engage them and help them achieve both functionally and critically. When we began working together he utilized very traditional teaching methods. When I asked why he utilized the methods he did, he stated he did so mostly to maintain control of the classroom. In our conversations, Mr. Delgado stated that he was reluctant to try new things for he didn't want to lose control of the class, and noted that the low readers and poor writers tended to be off-task when he gave them choices or broke from his routine. He felt a need to ensure they got the information they needed in order to pass the tests and be able to graduate. These stu-dents were placed in his class specifically, as he was identified as the teacher who was able to work with the low-performing students. Yet he feels at his best he can keep them on task, but felt powerless to help them learn to read the content both functionally and critically. Through our work together, Mr. Delgado did implement more student-centered techniques and began to see his classroom come to life as he gave up some of his routine and control and allowed students to work in pairs for processing and analyzing texts.

Levine (1995) states that the best way to challenge this depressing (though largely unacknowledged) reality of school tracking, whose metaphor is "school as factory," is with metaphors that seek to express our own counter vision of what schools should be. He suggests that the purpose of school should be "an experiment in democracy where students would be guided in developing values, skills, and knowledge needed to succeed in a democratic society" (p. 52). School should also be a place where teachers are viewed as artists rather than technicians. To achieve these goals would require us as teachers, along with our students, to actively confront the effects of racism, sexism, and class bias on student achievement through ongoing debate and a dialogue of praxis. What better place to begin such dialogue than within the literacy curriculum, where reading the word can be linked with reading the world. Finally, such an effort would result in a curriculum of high expectations for all that values and promotes student cooperation and individual thought and initiative; and as such would allow for all school curriculum to return to its root of *currere*, providing the space for students and teachers to journey actively into, through, and beyond the worn tracks and oppressive structures of ability groups. Such thinking leads us to empowerment and possibilities for change, not only in literacy but in all school curricula.

Engaging Critical Literacy

Only through communication can human life hold meaning. The teacher's thinking is authenticated only by the authenticity of the students' thinking (Freire, 1993, p. 58).

In response to institutional practices such as tracking and conservative ideological policies and views toward literacy, many teachers and researchers (e.g., Darder, 1991; Shor, 1992; Bartolome, 1994; Bigelow, 1998; Christensen, 1998; Greene, 1998) have responded by articulating critical practices and policies for literacy and bilingual education. This leads to "a different definition of literacy—one that acknowledges the hegemonic power structure and that values the discourses of groups that traditionally have been marginalized" (Powell, 1999, p. 20). Critical teachers and teacher researchers have begun to rise to this challenge, as I have attempted as well through my own teaching, research, and writing. These critical teachers and educators value student voice, linguistic diversity, cultural pluralism, and democratic schooling and emphasize literacy and biliteracy as processes of empowerment.

Critical educators support and promote the creation of critical literacy curriculums and classrooms where student voices, experiences, and histories are recognized and applied as a valued ingredient of the course content. At the core of such practice, or praxis, is Paulo Freire's concept of *consciensization*—the ability of teachers to take on both exposition and explanation as elements of critical dialogue (Freire, 1998). And, as such, teachers provide critical classroom activities that "help students analyze their own experiences so as to illuminate the processes by which those experiences were produced, legitimated, or disconfirmed" (McLaren, 1998, p. 217). In such an engagement, teachers are no longer dispensers of knowledge promoting only one canon or belief, but become agents of change in assisting students in seeing themselves within the larger historical, political, cultural, and economic structures where student voices do exist.

I advocate for participatory problem posing as one methodology and teaching process that can be utilized to transform academic knowledge into themes accessible to students. Such a curriculum "involves a two-way transformation of subject matter and discourse" (Shor, 1992, p. 77). In such classrooms, the subject matter is introduced by the teacher as a problem for students to reflect on in their own language. In presenting the curriculum in this manner, students—who come to class with their own universe of words, themes, and experiences—are challenged to go beyond themselves into a new territory not generated from their backgrounds. As a result, the role of the teacher is that of a democratic problem poser (Freire, 1993; Shor, 1992). The following is one example of how two educators put critical problem posing into practice in an inner-city high school English class.

In Linda Christensen's (1998) high school English class, students blamed themselves and/or their teachers for their poor performance on the PSATs. One student stated, "Well, if you'd taught us subject-verb agreement instead of writing, I'd have a better score on the verbal section" (p. 41). Rather than let such comments go, Christensen and her colleague, Bill Bigelow, asked students to write about a test they had taken. Both teachers also wrote papers on the topic as well. The following day the students and teachers read their papers to the class while seated in a circle. By doing this the teachers became part of the community, and as Christensen (1998) states, "If we didn't write and share, we would hold ourselves above and beyond the community we are trying to establish" (p. 41). The members of the community noted common themes among the stories and then began to question why they all came away from their testing experiences feeling threatened and stupid. The teachers felt that while the students could see similarities across experiences in the class, there was little solace because now they all felt they should/could have done better. This is the place where, I believe, most educators leave such discussions and, in doing so, fail students and perpetuate the hegemonic structures of ability groupings.

However, these teachers saw immediately that the students needed "a broader context in which to locate their feelings ... they needed to explore where these so-called aptitude and achievement tests originated and whose interests they served" (Christensen, 1998, p. 43). In response to this, Christensen and Bigelow introduced students to the creators of intelligence testing through books and writings on IQ and Educational Testing Service (ETS) testing histories and philosophies. From these readings students maintained dialogue journals and completed a historical study of standardized testing. Some facts the students discovered were that "SAT questions measured access to upper-class experience, not ability to make appropriate analogies" and the "vocabulary did not reflect the everyday experience of these inner-city kids" (p. 45). This lesson shows how students were able to engage in dialogue and research and begin to reveal hegemonic structures and, as a result, were able to see more clearly how the test did not take into consideration their individual experiences or lead students to an awareness of what knowledge was required to pass such exams.

Christensen (1998) points out that while this activity allowed students to "break down their sense of isolation and alienation, while they pushed toward a greater knowledge of how this society functions, they were moved less often to hope and action and more often to awareness and despair" (p. 46). This observation is critical because, while the teacher felt this was a positive activity, she was able to recognize that in order to foster change and empowerment among students, further interrogation was required. Christensen met with her colleague and engaged in a dialogue about how the lesson could be applied in the future and together they determined that in another lesson she could "put kids in touch with real people who haven't lost their hope, who still fight and plan to win" (p. 46).

Such praxis and consciensization on the part of the educators in this lesson is one key to implementing a critical literacy curriculum in the classroom. This lesson further demonstrates that reflection must occur not only during the process of dialogue with students, but also beyond the lesson, with other educators. In this manner, real change and empowerment can and does occur. However, being able to negotiate the realities of student achievement and critical praxis is not always an easy task. Below are several excerpts from my conversations with Mr. Clark, a teacher who functions from a critical ideological perspective. We were discussing the fact that his beginning-level ESL students were not performing well on the standardized grammar and writing tests that are part of the school requirement. Mr. Clark took issue with imposing a functional curriculum on students; he states:

> Well I, you know, I would—I would not agree with giving them [a text-based] dialogue because that's again, that's imposing something on them. And it's, you know, the only way that I have them speak English, is by presenting, doing a lot of presentations [on topics critical to them].

When I ask him what teaching is, he says,

> For me teaching is knowing [how] to practice it ... knowing when to move at the right moment. I learn this each year. There are ... learning spaces [that] are structured, for me the learning happens in relation, year by year.

Mr. Clark continues, "If there was reflection all along there would be a much more synchronous way [of learning] instead of feeling like it's too late." Here he is referring to the timeline of standardized tests and the pressure to have students ready to perform. He goes on to state that "there's not the time to think to establish my own system in the class ... I really wish they [system] would take the time to think, to support this [reflective practice] ... and also in my practice. I just think as teachers and for teachers and the people after us we just have to fight for that [reflective practice]."

I agree with Mr. Clark and note that we often are not trained to have such dialogue and even if we were, the school does not provide the space or time for teachers to meet to discuss such issues. He responds to the real tension he faces:

> So, even if as a teacher I profess a more dialectical way of teaching you know, and critical thinking, etc., it's still the way it's done ... at the block of time, the block of time is given, 8 or 7 hours for the students ... it's, it's banking, you know.

The transcript of our exchange that followed this comment illustrates a process of dialogue and reflection. In trying to help Mr. Clark to find a way, to define how to teach what needs to be taught without using a banking curriculum uncritically, and to more importantly value his resistance to the methods that tend to silence and control students.

K. Cadiero-Kaplan: Well, it's not totally banking [teaching skills] because … I mean the system is banking—we can't get away from that.

Mr. Clark: Yeah, that's what I mean the system is [banking] …

K. Cadiero-Kaplan: The system is, but what you have to figure out is how can I work within that system and keep my values as part of it? And one of things I found about you is that your values are very much a part of what you do and you recognize that. And you consciously try to keep that a part of it [what you teach] …you know your value for the critical thinking, for students being socially aware, for being able to speak up for themselves.

Mr. Clark: Hmmm.

K. Cadiero-Kaplan: And all of those things, and have a voice. You're struggling to empower them, but at the same time you're working within this banking system that says by this amount of time you have to have this, this, and this done. So that's where I think if you look at a balance … I think sometimes we can have congruency between what we believe and what we do, but without bringing the students to where they need to be.

Mr. Clark: Right.

K. Cadiero-Kaplan: So, then there has to be reflection back … on saying here are some ways I don't believe in teaching … like using grammar drills or using dialogues, but if those can be integrated at certain times [consciously]—

Mr. Clark: Then that's going to help [move the student up within the system]—

K. Cadiero-Kaplan: And find a way to either engage those [functional skills], maybe not in the way they are structured [in the texts], but be aware that they [the skills/functions] need to be a piece of your teaching language.

Mr. Clark: Yeah!

K. Cadiero-Kaplan: Because, see, ultimately the students are responsible, at the end [to produce on exams].

Mr. Clark: Right—at the end for their [product].

K. Cadiero-Kaplan: So the best I think we can do is say, … if you're doing all banking then what happens is everything you believe is gone and you're just doing this to get them through [transmitting knowledge uncritically], and then they're not being empowered and all those other pieces don't come in. So what you have to do is strike a balance between this critical pedagogy and the functional literacy [products] that are required [by the system so students can pass].

Mr. Clark: Yes, you see it's what you just said that's important to me [for students to be successful]. It's recognizing that the students are responsible at the end for, you know, learning [specific knowledge] … which is banking, [without losing process].

This conversation reflects not only Mr. Clark's concerns and his thinking processes, but my reflection and thinking as well. In all the conversations I had with the many teachers I have worked with, I have come to learn and to be convinced even more that we need to have these thoughtful discussions in order to truly understand what is being imposed, how we respond, and how and why we may accept or reject the varying ways of learning and knowing. So rather than finding one answer, we find multiple answers and pose even more problems, which is at the heart of a critical practice.

Catherine Walsh (1996) sums up best the realities and challenges that critical literacy educators face when constructing and implementing curriculum that has as its focus the transformation of school curriculum and society:

> Really becoming involved in the reshaping of our society and schools is difficult not only for the work it entails but because it challenges us to deal with uncomfortable, threatening, tension-producing concerns that are personal as

well as social in nature. It necessitates a thoughtful consideration of our individual perspectives and positions including how they came to be as well as a thoughtful consideration of our pedagogy and practice in and out of the classroom. Such a process requires that as educators, we become more cognizant of the differences between our students and ourselves—racial, ethnic, cultural, economic, residential, and generational (growing up in today's world vs. when we were children) of the overt and hidden ways that some students' voices are trivialized and denied, and of the ways that the policies, relations and instructional, and language practices of our classrooms and school reproduce the power and ideology of the broader society" (Walsh, 1996, pp. 227–228).

It is my contention that in order to begin to unveil teachers' ideological beliefs and practices, where their concern is for student achievement and academic success, all forms of literacy need to be recognized for their value in promoting academic literacy achievement. Further, by positioning these ideological forms in a historical context it clarifies the political forces that have influenced and continue to influence, educational pedagogy in regards to literacy and biliteracy.

So while all practices have value pedagogically, and while teachers are fluent in discussing practice and pedagogy, they are not always aware of the political and ideological orientations that frame their beliefs, teaching processes, or the curriculum materials they use. It is my hope that this text will be utilized to (a) inform teachers and educators about the political influences within the literacy curriculum, (b) assist teachers and educators in recognizing the utility of all the various forms and processes that promote literacy for their students, and (c) provide a framework for analyzing current beliefs and classroom practices.

It is important to note, however, that it is the critical literacy perspective that provides teachers with the tools for analyzing literacy policy and practices. The reflective tools presented here are not to be utilized as a way of dismissing opposing ideologies and placing them in contention with each other, but as a way of naming them. By engaging in critical analysis, teachers can ensure that they are not marginalizing students when they are utilizing processes, such as functional strategies of decoding if they reveal the codes (Delpit, 1995) while interrogating their function. Such skill-based strategies are important and necessary for many students, but can and should not be taught at the expense of engaging student voice, history, and experience. The next chapter is designed to keep the dialogue continuing beyond this text and beyond this historical time, for it is my desire that teachers use this book and the reflective activities within it as a tool for empowerment and enlightenment.

Chapter 6
Creating Knowledge
Through Praxis

Knowledge is not simply what teachers teach but also the productive meanings that students [as well as teachers] in all their cultural and social difference, bring to class-rooms as part of the production of knowledge and the construction of personal and social identities (Giroux, 1988, p. 162).

In this section the goal of the conversation process is for teachers to express their beliefs about literacy instruction and how they do or do not perceive the engagement of their beliefs in their teaching and practice. What I propose and in which I will engage readers here, is to take up the process of praxis toward what Bartolome calls *ideological clarity*, where individuals work to identify the dominant society's explanations for existing literacy curricula, the societal and political hierarchy that informs it, and their own beliefs and practices in literacy development. Bartolome (2000) asserts that

> ideological clarity requires that teacher's individual explanations be compared and contrasted with those propagated by the dominant society. It is to be hoped that the juxtaposing of ideologies forces teachers to better understand if, when, and how their belief systems uncritically reflect those of the dominant society and support unfair and inequitable conditions (p. 168).

By engaging in a critical examination of the political and ideological clarity in the area of literacy in particular, teachers can understand that they either "maintain the status quo, or they can work to transform the sociocultural" definitions of what it means to be a literate person and a teacher of literacy (Bartolome, 2000).

To begin this critical dialogue I will ask the reader to first reflect on his or her own beliefs about literacy using the Literacy Web depicted in

Figure 3. The web was created based on eight themes reflected in the literature as areas that influence and impact the teaching of literacy in schools, and which concern the definition, strategy, curriculum, and process of literacy, which is the center of the web. The eight themes include: definition of literacy, parent involvement, teaching strategies, collaboration, curriculum resources, student achievement, accountability and transition, and instructional goals.

Before going further each reader should take some time to reflect on these concepts as they relate or reflect their own beliefs and practice regarding literacy development for students and themselves. These eight areas are not defined specifically at this point, as it is imperative that each individual constructs his or her own responses and discuss how these terms are understood and defined both individually and collectively. Please feel free to use the graphic organizer to make notes or simply to reflect in thought or in a journal; there is no requirement to write. The point of the web is to provide a focus and context for the conversations that will follow.

Figure 3: Literacy Web

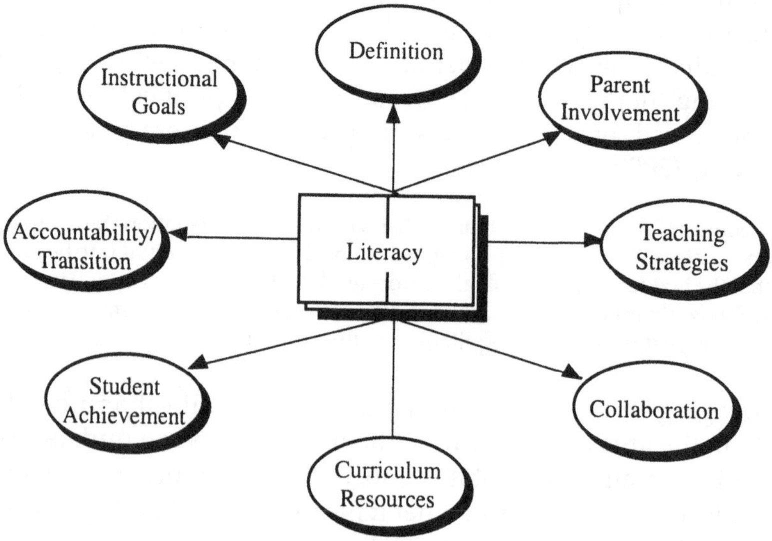

Praxis: Group Dialogue, Reflection & Action

After considering your own definitions and beliefs about literacy you can now work in small groups to discuss how you responded. Listed in Table 4, Literacy Web Questions, are the questions on which the table was based; you may use these questions to facilitate your group dialogue.

In order to achieve praxis you will also examine your beliefs and practices in the context of the Literacy Ideology & Policy Framework presented in Table 1, Chapter 2. As part of this process you want to identify areas of congruency and incongruence—that is, how does your ideology of literacy, your beliefs, match up with your actual practice? The school curriculum? The district standards? Part of this process is also identifying the ideology of the practice alongside your personal ideology.

Table 4: Literacy Web Questions

- What is your definition of literacy?
- What form of literacy do you feel is most important for your ELLs?
- How would you define biliteracy?
- How do you put into practice your ideas of literacy and illiteracy in your classroom?
- What do you expect your ELL students to accomplish by the end of the semester? school year? by graduation?
- What are your instructional goals for the school year for your ELL students?
- To achieve these goals, identify the curriculum resources and teaching strategies you utilize.
- How do you value professional development? What has been the most beneficial form of professional development you have received?
- How are you held accountable for the progress of your students?
- What forms of assessment do you use? How often?
- How do you determine a student's readiness to transition?
- Do you think parent involvement is important? If so, how do you accomplish this?
- What contributions do parents make to the literacy development of students?

After completing your conversations or dialogues, reflect back on your own web—what is the same or different? How has this conversation influenced your thinking on these issues?

Revisiting the Policy & Programming Framework

In Chapter 2 the reflection activity required that you consider eight areas impacting policy and programming for ELLs (Table 3); you also considered two key stakeholders in these processes—administrators and program coordinators. We will now revisit that initial reflection and expand it to include the teachers, students, parents, and the curriculum. The difference here will be that rather than reflecting on your thoughts regarding these issues, you will make critical observations. In this chapter I have used Table 3, the Framework for Examining Policy & Programming for English Language Learners (from Chapter 2), as the basis for an observational form, Table 5, School Curriculum & Program Review for ELLs. This review form can be used to consider the stakeholders, programming, and eight key program elements.

For each element try to objectively describe your school program, including teacher, parent, and student perspectives. The eight elements are the same—that is, value for learners, literacy orientation, instructional goals, resources (both financial and curricula), accountability and assessment, expectations for learners, and parent / community involvement—but are broken down into more specific observational categories. After completing your observations, present them to another stakeholder—a teacher, parent, or student—and ask him or her if he or she agrees or disagrees with your observations. The purpose here is to use this tool as a guide to examine your current school program and processes and identify areas for further examination, change, or growth. Such processes, however, cannot be engaged alone; they require thoughtful reflection, dialogue, and questioning with others, for praxis-like transformation cannot occur in isolation, but only in concert with others.

Component/ Stakeholder	Observations Based on School Site Visit & Interviews with key stake- holders, including administrators, program coordinators, teachers, students, parents, and curriculum review.	Scale 1 Minimal services/support 2 Basic services/support 3 Satisfactory services/support 4 Advanced services/support 5 Superior services/support
School Environment Initial Impressions		
1. Program Design & Approaches		
2. Value for Learners		
3. Expectations for Learners		
4. Instructional Goals		
5. Literacy Orientation		
6.1 Resources: Curriculum L1		

Table 5: School Curriculum & Program Review for ELLs

© Cadiero-Kaplan (2001).

6.2 Resources: Curriculum L2				
6.3 Resources: Professional Development				
7. Accountability & Assessment: Instructional				
8. Parent Involvement/ Engagement				
Other:				

Table 5 (cont.): School Curriculum & Program Review for ELLs

© Cadiero-Kaplan (2001).

1. Program Approaches: Question: How does the program approach at the school supports or interacts with literacy development, instructional goals, value for learners, and academic achievement? (Program Types: English Only, Sheltered Immersion, Early Exit, Late Exit, Dual Language)

2. Value for Learners: Question: How are ELLs are viewed within the policy and program and by concerned stakeholders (i.e., teachers, administrators, parents, and students)? Areas of concentration include learners as valued participants in the learning process; valued for being bilingual, biliterate, or learning English. Visible indicators present in the school context.

3. Expectations for Learners: Question: How do schools identify the expectations of students as defined by the stakeholders, policy, and programs? For example, by graduation what are the students expected to be able to do and/or accomplish, including expectations and methods of preparedness?

4. Instructional Goals: Question: What is the value that is placed on literacy? Is there recognition for various forms of literacy and language learning? This dimension seeks to identify the multiple forms of literacy that are important and/or valued at the school site.

5. Literacy Orientation: Question: What is the value that is placed on literacy? Is there recognition for various forms of literacy and language learning? This dimension seeks to identify the multiple forms of literacy that are important and/or valued at the school site.

6.1 Resources - Curriculum in L1: Question: How do schools identify and evaluate the curriculum resources and their use on-site and in the classroom in the first language?

6.1 Resources - Curriculum in L2: Question: How do schools identify and evaluate the curriculum resources and their use on-site and in the classroom in the second language?

6.3 Resources - Professional Development: Question: How do schools identify and evaluate the human resources that are allocated/dedicated to programming and curricula for ELLs? Included here are personnel resources, the capacity of teaching staff and materials utilized in curriculum development.

7.1 Accountability & Assessment - Instructional: Question: How do schools determine the level of accountability of not only student achievement and success, but program implementation, transition to English, testing in L1 and L2, and the accountability levels of those responsible for the process?

7.2 Accountability & Assessment - Instructional: Question: How do schools determine the level of accountability to funding sources as well as funds allocated to assessment and evaluation?

8. Parent Involvement/Engagement: Question: How do schools identify and evaluate how parents are valued, involved, and engaged in school activities? How does collaboration between home and school take place?

Table 5 (cont.): School Curriculum & Program Review for ELLs

© Cadiero-Kaplan (2001).

Afterword:
The Journey Begins

We need to recognize that what we single out as most deficient and oppressive is in part a function of perspectives created by our past. It is a past in which our subjectivities are embedded, whether we are conscious of it or not. We have reached a point when that past must be reinterpreted and reincarnated in the light of what we have learned (Greene, 1996, p. 28).

The manner in which the silencing or devaluing of teacher and student voices occurs is oftentimes below our own levels of awareness. Through teacher credential programs and staff development, teachers are taught methods and teaching techniques, but rarely examine issues of ideology. They believe that if they are utilizing methods or materials designed to teach their students the required skills and processes they need, then as teachers they are doing a good job and the right thing by their students. As well, teachers are often told and believe that "the solution to the current underachievement of students from subordinated cultures is often reduced to finding the 'right' teaching methods, strategies, or prepackaged curricula that will work" (Bartolome, 1996, p. 230). I contend that what experienced teachers need is not more methods and strategies, but the time, opportunity, and educational space to analyze their curriculum and practice in the context of their beliefs, critical theory, and the larger sociopolitical context. That is, to be given the opportunity and language to critically analyze the sociopolitical agendas linked with certain ideologies, pedagogy, and teaching processes, and to respond accordingly on an individual and collective basis, in the work toward ideological clarity. However, as stated earlier, without the space to explore such critical issues, without support from school administrators, and without critical teacher education classes and programs, such processes are not likely to occur unless teachers, teacher educators, and even students, parents, and community members demand and actively seek these avenues. It is my hope that this text will serve as a resource that can be utilized in the creation of spaces where such critical dialogical processes can begin. Further, it is my desire that such dialogue will lead to the development of more research that is grounded in the everyday reality of schools and society, conducted by teachers in collaboration with parents, community members, and university researchers. For this is where I began, and in so doing we need to recognize that, "Social scientists are human beings who have both minds and hearts ... The hearts of social scientists exercise a cogent influence on research questions, findings, concepts, generalizations, and theories (Banks, 1988, pp. 4–5).

My initial research that informed this book came out of my desire to work in the schools in which I learned and taught, to talk directly and honestly with high school teachers and students in their language, their world and words. During the early stages of this project I talked with many high school students who were deemed illiterate in both their native language and English, even though they could speak fluently in two or more languages. What was more surprising to me was that their teachers did not seem disturbed by the fact that these students were not academically proficient in either language. The teachers were very matter-of-fact when they stated that many would just barely graduate from high school, never mind attending college. This attitude, from seemingly caring and professional teachers, surprised and saddened me.

I was reminded of my own experiences as a marginalized high school student. I was reminded how teachers expected that I would become an office manager or clerk because I didn't have the potential to apply or attend even the local state colleges, and how my high school counselor dismissed my thoughts of college so readily. I further reflected on my own teaching experiences and the challenges my students and I had to overcome on a daily basis. I recalled teacher colleagues who felt my methods were inappropriate and didn't understand how I could stimulate students, who wouldn't read or write in their classes, to become interested in reading Edgar Allen Poe and John Steinbeck, the regular high school curriculum. They questioned how I could motivate these seemingly underperforming students to write for a school newspaper, use computers to do research, and write poetry and short stories.

Thus, with my own experiences as student and teacher as the vehicle, I was even more determined to find out how teachers who cared about students could so readily dismiss those whom they felt were at the end of the line. I felt that the system had a hand in the attitudes these various teachers held.

Through these very personal experiences and deep reflection I knew I wanted to work directly in schools with teachers and develop research with them so that we could learn together, and then ultimately contribute what we learned to the field of education; to contribute work that would validate the experiences of teachers like me and the students we taught and continue to teach. I wanted to focus on literacy development for bilingual students who are continually marginalized and impacted by federal, state, and local policies and oftentimes end up in special education classrooms. Policies that are determined not by teachers like me and my peers, but by uncritical teachers, voters, businessmen, and the myriad of politicians who are mostly monolingual and reflect the white, middle-class majority.

When I began this research several years ago I was looking for answers and was trying to understand how literacy views came to be determined and then validated, not just within English curricula but in bilingual education as well. I believed when I started, and still do, that in order to improve literacy and bilingual education, we, as teachers and educators, need to focus policy and research agendas on literacy and toward clarifying definitions of literacy and biliteracy. It is only then, through this process, that we can reveal and dismantle the ideological positions that historically and habitually marginalize individuals within the existing educational policies for literacy and bilingual education. I have come to realize that in order to begin this transformation, teachers and parents need to start to work together across school grade levels and programs. That is, teachers from mainstream classrooms to ESL classes, bilingual classrooms, and special education classes need to have critical dialogue about issues of ideology, language, and literacy, because as teachers we all teach literacy. We need to collaboratively work toward a system dedicated to quality education for all students, a system that focuses on an individual's needs within society, not society's needs for individuals.

My research and this book emerged from a resonant personal experience, and like an orchestral symphony its composition slowly became a part of my day, in harmony with the greater part of my life. While I realize the significance of this work to the field of education, I also cannot dismiss the significance this work has had on my life. I was able to create a study, live a process, and ultimately write a book that emerged from my heart and allowed me to speak more credibly about my passions for literacy, teaching, equity, and social justice. I was able to take this work to teachers I work with both in schools and at the university and now to you, the reader of this text. As part of this journey, which is never-ending, I have begun to be able to read the world and the word, surrounded by all who travel this complex path. I do believe we are all travelers trying to make sense of our place in the world; we not only learn from and teach each other, but we each create and re-create the road by walking—so let's walk together and embrace diversity in all its colors, forms, languages, tensions, and contradictions.

> *Caminante no hay camino,*
> *se hace el camino al andar*
>
> Traveler, there is no road.
> The road is made as one walks.
> —Antonio Machado

Appendix
Resources: Web-Based Resources & References for Critical Literacy Curriculum Development

California Consortium for Critical Educators: *http://www.ccce.net*
The California Consortium for Critical Educators (CCCE) is a social movement established with an expressed commitment to serve critical educators, as well as the students, parents, and communities we touch each day through our labor. Toward this end, we embrace our human differences as workers and citizens of the world, as we work to advance the reconstruction of schooling and society.

Freedom Archives: *http://www.freedomarchives.org/index.html*
The Freedom Archives contain over 5,000 hours of audiotapes. These recordings date from the late-1960s to the mid-1990s and chronicle the progressive history of the Bay Area, the United States, and international solidarity movements. The collection includes weekly news, poetry, music programs broadcast on several educational radio stations; in-depth interviews and reports on social and cultural issues; diverse activist voices; original and recorded music, poetry, original sound collages; and an extensive La Raza collection.

Global Exchange: *http://www.globalexchange.org/*
Global Exchange is an international human rights organization dedicated to promoting environmental, political, and social justice. Since our founding in 1988, we have increased the US public's global awareness while building partnerships worldwide.

National Council of Teachers of English: *http://www.ncte.org*
The National Council of Teachers of English is devoted to improving the teaching and learning of English and the language arts at all levels

of education. Since 1911, NCTE has provided a forum for the profession, an array of opportunities for teachers to continue their professional growth throughout their careers, and a framework for cooperation to deal with issues that affect the teaching of English. The Council promotes the development of literacy, the use of language to construct personal and public worlds and to achieve full participation in society, through the learning and teaching of English and the related arts and sciences of language.

Pacific Southwest Regional Technology in Ed Consortium:
http://psrtec.clmer.csulb.edu/
PSR*TEC is one of six U.S. Department of Education-funded Regional Technology in Education Consortia helping to integrate advanced technologies into K–12 teaching and learning and adult literacy. Our lead agency is the Center for Language Minority Education and Research, based at California State University, Long Beach. We work with educators and community members on developing access to and meaningful uses of advanced technologies for education reform, school renewal, and the development of technology-enhanced lifelong learning communities inside and outside of schools. Our fundamental purpose is to help implement the use of advanced technologies to improve learning and educational success to high standards for all students.

Public Agenda On-Line: *http://www.publicagenda.org/*
For over a quarter of a century, Public Agenda has been providing unbiased and unparalleled research that bridges the gap between American leaders and what the public really thinks about issues ranging from education to foreign policy to immigration to religion and civility in American life. Nonpartisan and nonprofit, Public Agenda was founded by social scientist and author Daniel Yankelovich and former Secretary of State Cyrus Vance in 1975. Public Agenda's two-fold mission is to help

- American leaders better understand the public's point of view.
- citizens know more about critical policy issues so they can make thoughtful, informed decisions.

Rethinking Schools On-Line: *http://www.rethinkingschools.org/*
Rethinking Schools began in 1986 as a local effort to address problems such as basal readers, standardized testing, and textbook-dominated curriculum. Throughout its history, Rethinking Schools has tried to

balance classroom practice and educational theory. It is an activist publication, with articles written by and for teachers, parents, and students. Yet it also addresses key policy issues, such as vouchers and marketplace-oriented reforms, funding equity, and school-to-work.

Rouge Forum: *http://www.pipeline.com/~rgibson/rouge_forum/*
The Rouge Forum is a group of educators, students, and parents seeking a democratic society. We are concerned about questions like these: How can we teach against racism, national chauvinism, and sexism in an increasingly authoritarian and undemocratic society? How can we gain enough real power to keep our ideals and still teach—or learn? Whose interests shall school serve in a society that is ever more unequal? We are both research and action oriented. We want to learn about equality, democracy, and social justice as we simultaneously struggle to bring into practice our present understanding of what that is. We seek to build a caring inclusive community which understands that an injury to one is an injury to all. At the same time, our caring community is going to need to deal decisively with an opposition that is sometimes ruthless.

Teaching to Change the World—Student Resources:
http://www.mhhe.com/socscience/education/oakes/student/links.mhtml
The goal of Teaching to Change the World is to help new teachers develop theories of learning and teaching based on sociocultural and critical learning principles and teaching practices suitable for democratic and inclusive classrooms. This website offers a wealth of resocures for developing critical curriculum and instruction.

Teaching to Change LA: UCLA Institute for Democracy, Education & Access: *http://tcla.gseis.ucla.edu/rights/*
Teaching to Change *LA* (TCLA) is an on-line journal that addresses educational conditions in Los Angeles schools. K–12 students, parents, teachers, guest contributors, and researchers provide the content for the journal, which is published eight times a year with weekly updates. Journal readers include those who learn and teach in Los Angeles schools, local and state policy makers and legislators, and readers from across the country.

TCLA creates a unique environment from which urban students, parents, and teachers can be heard beyond their local classrooms. Our contributors use computer-generated maps, photographs, graphs, video, and audio to communicate the complex ideas, stories, and other data that are relevant to their own communities and schools.

Truthout News & Politics: *http://www.truthout.org/*
Truthout provides readers with critical news and commentary on world events. Truthout currently reaches a quarter of a million readers per month. Our staff and volunteers have increased from one to eight in the last year. We have received a wonderful response from our readers who daily tell us that Truthout is providing them with valuable information.
Truthout provides this service free of charge and depends solely on donations from readers to meet expenses. This allows us to remain independent without any pressure to modify our editorial policy to please funding sources.

Z Net Magazine: *http://www.zmag.org*
Z Magazine's ZNet is a sophisticated website with diverse extra-web functionality but simple design and graphics for easy navigation. It is a continuous town meeting and intellectual and activist service center for large sectors of the progressive community. It is a place to

- get useful information
- exchange ideas
- develop new political programs and unity
- engage in on-line activism
- acclimate to and learn new technologies
- meet new people
- enjoy and educate yourself
- browse the WWW with extensive guidance

You won't find uncivil language or flaming, sexism, racism, or commercialism. What you will find is a community of people seeking to understand society and to change it for the better.

References

Adams, M. J. (1990). *Beginning to read: Thinking and learning about print*. Urbana-Champaign: Center for the Study of Reading at the University of Illinois.

Adams, J. (1995). Proposition 187 lessons. *Z Magazine 8* (3), 16–18.

Alexander, D., & Nava, A. (1976). *A public policy analysis of bilingual education in California*. San Francisco: R and E Research Associates.

Apple, M. (1979). *Ideology and curriculum*. New York: Routledge.

Apple, M. (1986). *Teachers and texts: A political economy of class & gender relations in education*. New York: Routledge.

Apple, M. (1995). *Education and power*. New York: Routledge.

Apple, M. (1996). *Cultural politics and education*. New York: Teachers College Press.

Arnstine, D. (1995). *Democracy and the arts of schooling*. New York: State University of New York Press.

Aronowitz, S., & Giroux, H. (1985). *Education under siege*. New York: Bergin & Garvey.

Aronowitz, S., & Giroux, H. (1991). *Postmodern education: Politics, culture & social criticism*. Minneapolis: University of Minnesota Press.

Au, K. H. (1998). Social constructivism and the school literacy learning of students of diverse backgrounds. *Journal of Literacy Research 30*, 297–319.

Auerbach, E. (1991). Literacy and ideology. *Annual Review of Applied Linguistics, 12*, 71–85.

August D., & Garcia, E. (1988). *Language minority education in the United States: Research, policy, and practice*. Springfield, IL: C. C. Thomas.

August, D., & Hakuta, K. (Eds.). (1997). *Improving schooling for language-minority children: A research agenda*. Washington, DC: National Academy Press.

Banks, J. A. (1998). The lives and values of researchers: Implications for educating citizens in a multicultural society. *Educational Researcher 27* (7), 4–17.

Baker, C. (1996). *Foundations of bilingual education and bilingualism* (2nd ed.). Philadelphia, PA: Multilingual Matters.

Bartolome, L. I. (1994). Teaching strategies: Their possibilities and limitations. In B. McLeod (Ed.), *Language and learning: Educating linguistically diverse students* (pp. 199–223). New York: State University of New York Press.

Bartolome, L. (1996). Beyond the methods fetish: Toward a humanizing pedagogy. In P. Leistyna, A. Woodrum, & S. Sherbloom (Eds.), *Breaking free. The transformative power of critical pedagogy* (pp. 229-252). Cambridge, MA: Harvard Educational Review.

Bartolome, L. (2000). Democratizing bilingualism: The role of critical teacher education. In Beyknot, Z. F. (Ed.), *Lifting every voice: Pedagogy and politics of bilingualism* (pp. 167-186). Boston, MA: Harvard Education Publishing Group.

Behuniak, P., Hubert, J., LaFontaine, H., & Nearine, R. (1988). *Bilingual education: Evaluation politics and practices. Evaluation Review 12* (5), 483–509.

Bennett, W. J. (Ed.). (1995). *The children's book of virtues.* Needham Heights, MA: Simon & Schuster Publishing.

Bigelow, B. (1998). The human lives behind the labels—The global sweatshop, niki, and the race to the bottom. In W. Ayers, J. Hunt, & T. Quinn (Eds.), *Teaching for social justice: A democracy and education reader* (pp. 21–38). New York: Teachers College Press.

Bloom, A. (1987). *The closing of the American mind: How higher education has failed democracy and impoverished the souls of today's students.* New York: Simon & Schuster.

Bogdan, R., & Biklen, S. K. (1992). *Qualitative research for education: An introduction to theory and methods* (2nd ed.). Boston, MA: Allyn & Bacon.

Bowles, S., & Gintes, H. (1971). *Schooling in capitalist America.* New York: Basic Books.

Brice-Heath, S. (1976). A national language academy? Debate in the new nation. *International Journal of the Sociology of Language 47* (11), 9–43.

Brice-Heath, S. (1983). *Ways with words: Language, life, and work in communities and classrooms.* New York: Cambridge University Press.

Brisk, M. (1998). *Bilingual education: From compensatory to quality schooling.* Mahwah, NJ: Lawrence Erlbaum Associates.

Brisk, M. E., & Harrington, M. (2000). *Literacy and Bilingualism: A handbook for all teachers.* Mahwah, NJ: Lawrence Erlbaum Associates.

Burke, F. G. (1981). Bilingualism/biculturalism in American education: An adventure in wonderland. *The Annals of the American Academy of Political and Social Science 454,* 164–177.

Cadiero-Kaplan, K. (2001). *Literacy ideology and practice: Teacher's beliefs and practices for English language learners at the secondary level.* San Diego, CA: Dissertation submitted to San Diego State University and Claremont Graduate University.

Cadiero-Kaplan, K. (2002). Literacy ideologies: Critically engaging the language arts curriculum. *Language Arts Journal 79* (5), 372–392.

California Consortium for Teacher Development. (1997). *Teacher education and credentialing for student diversity: The case in California.* Santa Cruz: University of California, Santa Cruz.

California Department of Education. (2002). *Language census* (form R30–LC). Sacramento, CA: Author. Available: http://www.ed-data.k12.ca.us/

Chamot, A. (1998). Effective instruction for high school English language learners. In R. Gersten & R. T. Jimenez (Eds.), *Promoting learning for culturally and linguistically diverse students* (pp. 187–209). Belmont, CA: Wadsworth Publishing.

Christensen, L. (1998). Writing the word and the world. In W. Ayers, J. Hunt, & T. Quinn (Eds.), *Teaching for social justice: A democracy and education reader* (pp. 39–47). New York: Teachers College Press.

Cochran-Smith, M., & Lytle, S. L. (1993). *Inside/outside teacher research and knowledge*. New York: Teachers College Press.

Cohen, P. (1982). *A calculating people: The spread of numeracy in early America*. Chicago, IL: University of Chicago Press.

Coles, G. (1998). *Reading lessons: The debate over literacy*. New York: Hill & Wang Publishers.

Coles, G. (2000). *Misreading reading: The bad science that hurts children*. Portsmouth, NH: Heinemann.

Collier, V. (1987). Age and rate of acquisition of second language for academic purposes. *TESOL Quarterly 21* (4), 617–641.

Cota, I. C. (1997). The role of previous educational learning experiences on current academic performance and second language proficiency of intermediate school limited English proficient students. *Bilingual Research Journal 21* (2 & 3), 103–118.

Courts, P. L. (1997). *Multicultural literacies: Dialect, discourse, and diversity*. New York: Peter Lang Publishing.

Cox, C. (1999). *Teaching language arts: A student- and response-centered classroom* (3rd ed.). Boston, MA: Allyn & Bacon.

Crawford, J. (1992). *Language loyalties: A source book on the official English controversy*. Chicago, IL: University of Chicago Press.

Crawford, J. (1999). *Bilingual education: History, politics, theory, and practice* (4th ed.). Los Angeles: Bilingual Educational Services.

Cummins, J. (1989). *Empowering minority students*. Sacramento: California Association for Bilingual Education.

Cummins, J. (1994). Primary language instruction and the education of language minority students. In C. F. Leyba (Ed.), *Schooling and language minority students: A theoretical framework* (pp. 3–49). Los Angeles: Evaluation Dissemination and Assessment Center, California State University, Los Angeles.

Darder, A. (1991). *Culture and power in the classroom: A critical foundation for bicultural education*. Westport, CT: Bergin & Garvey.

Darder, A. (2002). *Reinventing Paulo Freire: A pedagogy of love*. Boulder, CO: Westview Press.

Delpit, L. (1995). *Other people's children*. New York: The New Press.

Dewey, J. (1904). *The relation of theory to practice in education: The third NSSE yearbook* (pt. 1). Chicago, IL: Chicago University Press.

Dewey, J. (1916). *Democracy and education*. New York: Free Press.

Dewey, J. (1944). *Democracy and education*. New York: Free Press.

Dewey, J. (1959). *Dewey on education: Selections*. R. Archambault (Ed.). New York: Teachers College Press.

Dolch, E. L. (1950). *Teaching primary reading*. Champaign, IL: Garrard.

Edelsky, C., Altwerger, B., & Flores, B. (1991). *Whole language: What's the difference?* Portsmouth, NH: Heinemann.

Eisner, E. (1994). *The educational imagination: On the design and evaluation of school programs* (3rd ed.). New York: MacMillan Publishers.

Escobedo, D. (1999). Propositions 187 and 227: Latino immigrant rights to education. *Human Rights Magazine* (summer), 13–15.

Espinosa, R. (2000). [Repertoire of teaching strategies]. Unpublished data collection form.

Espinosa, R., & Ochoa, A. (1995). The educational attainment of California youth: A research note. In R. Macias & R. Garcia Ramon (Eds.), *Changing schools for changing students: An anthology of research on language minorities, schools & society.* Santa Barbara: University of California Linguistic Minority Research Institute Publication.

Estrada, L. J. (1979). A chronicle of the political, legislative and judicial advances for bilingual education in California and the American southwest. In R. V. Padilla (Ed.), *Bilingual education and public policy in the United States* (pp. 97–108). Ypsilanti: Eastern Michigan University, Department of Foreign Languages and Bilingual Studies.

Faltis, C. J. (1999). Creating a new history. In C. J. Faltis & P. Wolfe (Eds.), *So much to say: Adolescents, bilingualism, and ESL in the secondary school* (pp. 1–12). New York: Teachers College Press.

Faltis, C. J., & Wolfe, P. (1999). *So much to say: Adolescents, bilingualism, and ESL in the secondary school.* New York: Teachers College Press.

Forester, J. (1988). *Critical theory and public life.* Cambridge, MA: MIT Press.

Foucault, M. (1977). *Power/knowledge.* New York: Pantheon Books.

Freire, P. (1993). *Pedagogy of the oppressed.* New York: Continuum Publishing.

Freire, P. (1998). *Pedagogy of freedom: Ethics, democracy and civic discourse.* New York: Rowan & Littlefield Publishers.

Freire, P., & Macedo, D. (1987). *Literacy: Reading the word and the world.* Westport, CT: Bergin & Garvey.

Freire, P., & Shor, I. (1987). *A pedagogy for liberation: Dialogues on transforming education.* South Hadley, MA: Bergin & Garvey.

Galindo, R. (1997). Language wars: The ideological dimensions of the debates on bilingual education. *Bilingual Research Journal 21* (2 & 3), 103–141.

Garcia, E. (1993). *Education of linguistically and culturally diverse students: Effective instructional practices.* Educational Report No. 1. Santa Cruz, CA: National Center for Research on Cultural Diversity and Second Language Learning.

Garcia, G. E., Stephens, D. L., Koenke, K. R., Harris, V. J., Pearson, P. D., Jimenez, R. T., & Janisch, C. (1995). *Reading instruction and educational opportunity at the middle school level* (Tech. Report No. 622). Urbana-Champaign: University of Illinois, Center for the Study of Reading.

Gee, J. P. (1990). *Social linguistics and literacies: Ideology in discourses.* New York: The Falmer Press.

Giroux, H. (1981). *Ideology, culture, and the process of schooling.* Philadelphia, PA: Temple University Press.

Giroux, H. (1983). *Theory and resistance in education: A pedagogy for the opposition.* Granby, MA: Bergin & Garvey.

Giroux, H. (1985). Introduction. In P. Freire, *The politics of education: Culture, power and liberation* (pp. xi–xxv). South Hadley, MA: Bergin & Garvey.

Giroux, H. (1987). Introduction: Literacy and the pedagogy of political empowerment. In P. Freire & D. Macedo, *Literacy, reading the word and the world* (pp. 1–27). Westport, CT: Bergin & Garvey.

Giroux, H. (1988). *Schooling and the struggle for public life: Critical pedagogy in the modern age.* Minneapolis: University of Minnesota Press.

Giroux, H. (1996). *Living dangerously: Multiculturalism and the politics of difference.* New York: Peter Lang Publishing.

Goodman, K. (1986). Poor readers don't get to read much in reading groups. *Language Arts, 57* (8) p. 873-875.

Goodman, K. S. (1986). *What's whole in whole language?* Portsmouth, NH: Heinemann.

Goodman, K., Shannon, P., Murphy, Y., & Freeman, S. (1988). *Report card on basal readers.* Katonah, NY: R. C. Owen.

Gramsci, A. (1971). *Selections from Prison Notebooks.* New York: International Publications.

Greene, M. (1996). In search of a critical pedagogy. In P. Leistyna, A. Woodrum, & S. Sherbloom (Eds.), *Breaking free: The transformative power of critical pedagogy (pp. 13-30).* Cambridge, MA: Harvard Educational Review.

Greene, M. (1998). Introduction: Teaching for social justice. In W. Ayers, J. Hunt, & T. Quinn (Eds.), *Teaching for social justice: A democracy and education reader* (pp. xxvii-xlvi). New York: Teachers College Press.

Hakuta, K. (1986). *Mirror of language: The debate on bilingualism.* New York: Basic Books.

Hallin, D. (1988). The American news media: A critical theory perspective. In J. Forester (Ed.), *Critical theory and public life* (pp. 121–146). Cambridge, MA: MIT Press.

Hamayan, E. V. (1994). Language development of low-literacy students. In F. Genesee (Ed.), *Educating second language children: The whole child, the whole curriculum, the whole community* (pp. 278–300). New York: Cambridge University Press.

Harman, S, & Edelsky, C. (1989). The risks of whole language literacy: Alienation and connection. *Language Arts 66* (4), 392–406.

Hernandez-Chavez, E. (1988). Language policy and language rights in the United States: Issues in bilingualism. In T. Skutnabb-Kangas & J. Cummins (Eds.), *Minority education: From shame to struggle* (pp. 45–56). Philadelphia, PA: Multilingual Matters Ltd.

Hinchey, P. (1998). *Finding freedom in the classroom: A practical introduction to critical theory.* New York: Peter Lang Publishing.

Hirsch, E. D. (Ed.). (1988). *Cultural literacy: What every American needs to know.* New York: Vintage Books.

Hobson, E., & Shuman, R. B. (1990). *Reading and writing in high schools: A whole-language approach.* Washington, DC: National Education Association.

Hollingsworth, S., & Gallego, M. (1996). Toward a collaborative praxis of multiple literacies. *Curriculum Inquiry 26* (3), 265–292.

Holt, J. (1967). *How children learn.* New York: Pitman.

Horton, J., & Calderon, J. (1992). Language struggles in a changing California community. In J. Crawford (Ed.), *Language loyalties: A source book on the official English controversy in the United States* (pp. 186–194). Chicago, IL: University of Chicago Press.

Kanoon, G. D. (1978). The four phases of bilingual education in the United States. *TESOL Newsletter 12* (2), 1, 23–24.

Kelly, U. A. (1997). *Schooling desire: Literacy, cultural politics, and pedagogy.* New York: Routledge.

Kemmis, S., & Wilkson, M. (1998). Participatory action research and the study of practice. In B. Atweh, S. Kemmis, & P. Weeks (Eds.), *Action research in practice: Partnership for social justice* (pp. 21–36). London: Routledge.

Kerper-Mora, J. (2000a). Policy shifts in language minority education: A mismatch between politics and pedagogy. *The Educational Forum 64* (3), 204–214.

Kerper-Mora, J. (2000b). *Proposition 227's Second Anniversary: Triumph or Travesty?* Available: http://coe.sdsu.edu/people/jmora/ Prop227/227YearTwo.htm

Kincheloe, J. (1995). Meet me behind the curtain: The struggle for a critical postmodern action research. In P. L. McLaren & J. M. Giarelli (Eds.), *Critical theory and educational research* (pp. 71–89). New York: State University of New York Press.

Kincheloe, J. (1998). Pinar's currere and identity in hyperreality: Grounding the post-formal notion of intrapersonal intelligence. In W. Pinar (Ed.), *Curriculum towards new identities* (pp. 129–142). New York: Garland Press.

Kincheloe, J. (2003). Critical ontology: Vision of selfhood and curriculum. *Journal of Curriculum Theorizing 19* (1), pp 47–64.

Knoblauch, C. H., & Brannon, L. (1993). *Critical teaching and the idea of literacy*. Portsmouth, NH: Heinemann.

Kozol, J. (1991). *Savage inequalities: Children in America's schools*. New York: Crown Publishers.

Krashen, S. D. (1993). *The power of reading: Insights from the research*. Englewood, CO: Libraries Unlimited, Inc.

Krashen, S. D. (1994). Bilingual education and second language acquisition theory. In C. F. Leyba (Ed.), *Schooling and language minority students: A theoretical framework* (pp. 51–79). Los Angeles: Evaluation Dissemination and Assessment Center, California State University, Los Angeles.

Krashen, S., & Terrell, T. (1983). *The natural approach: Language acquisition in the classroom*. Englewood Cliffs, NJ: Alemany/Prentice Hall.

Lapp, D., & Flood, J. (1983). *Teaching every child to read* (3rd ed.). New York: Macmillan Publishing.

Leibowitz, A. H. (1984). The official character of language in the United States: Literacy requirements for immigration, citizenship, and entrance into American life. *Aztlan 15* (1), 25–70.

Leistyna, P., Woodrum, A., & Sherblom, S. (1996). *Breaking free: The transformative power of critical pedagogy*. Cambridge, MA: Harvard Educational Review.

Levine, D. (1995). Building a vision of curriculum reform. In D. Levine, R. Lowe, B. Peterson, & R. Tenorio (Eds.), *Rethinking schools: An agenda for change* (pp. 52–60). New York: The New Press.

Luke, A. (1988). *Literacy, textbooks and ideology: Postwar literacy instruction and the mythology of Dick and Jane*. New York: The Falmer Press.

Lusted, D. (1986). Why Pedagogy. *Screen 27*, 5.

Macedo, D. (1991). The politics of an emancipatory literacy in Cape Verde. In C. Mitchell & K. Weiler (Eds.), *Rewriting literacy: Culture and the discourse of the other* (pp. 147–160). Westport, CT: Bergin & Garvey.

Macedo, D. (1994). *Literacies of power: What Americans are not allowed to know*. San Francisco: Westview Press.

Macedo, D., Dendrinos, B., & Gounari, P. (2003). *The hegemony of English*. Boulder, CO: Paradigm Publishers.

Macias, Reynaldo F. (1989). Bilingualism, language contact, and immigrant languages. *Annual Review of Applied Linguistics 10*, 13–25.

Machado, A. (1982). *Selected Poems*. Translated by Alan S. Trueblood. Proverb "se hace camino al andar," p. 143. Cambridge, MA: Harvard University Press.

Malakoff, M., & Hakuta, K. (1990). History of language minority education in the United States. In A. Padilla, H. Fairchild, & C. Valadez (Eds.), *Bilingual education: Issues and strategies* (pp. 27–43). London: Sage Publications.

Matthews, M. (2000). Electronic literacy and the limited English proficient student. *Reading Online*. May. Available: http://www.readingonline. org/electronic/matthews/index.html

McKay, S. (1993). Agendas for second language literacy. New York: Cambridge University Press.

McLaren, P. (1988). Culture of canon? Critical pedagogy and the politics of literacy. *Harvard Educational Review 58* (2), 213–234.

McLaren, P. (1998). *Life in schools: An introduction to critical pedagogy in the foundations of education*. New York: Longman Press.

Merriam, S. B. (1998). *Qualitative research and case study applications in education*. San Francisco: Jossey-Bass.

Miles, M., & Huberman, A. M. (1994). *Qualitative data analysis: An expanded sourcebook* (2nd ed.). Thousand Oaks, CA: Sage Publications.

Minicucci, C., & Olsen, L. (1992). *Programs for secondary limited English proficient students: A California study*. Washington, DC: National Clearinghouse for Bilingual Education.

Montaner, C. A. (1992). Talk English—You are in the United States. In J. Crawford (Ed.), *Language loyalties: A source book on the official English controversy in the United States* (pp. 163–165). Chicago, IL: University of Chicago Press.

Mouffe, C. (1979). Hegemony and ideology. In Gramsci C. Mouffee (Ed.), *Gramsci & Marxist Theory*. Boston: Routledge & Kegan Press.

Murnane, R., & Levy, F. (1996). *Teaching the new basic skills: Principles of educating children to thrive in a changing economy*. New York: Free Press.

Myers, M. (1996). *Changing our minds: Negotiating English and literacy*. Urbana, IL: National Council of Teachers of English.

Nicaise, M., & Barnes, D. (1996). The union of technology, constructivism, and teacher education. *Journal of Teacher Education 47* (3), 205–212.

Nieto, S. (1996). I like making my mind work: Language minority students and the curriculum. In C. Walsh (Ed.), *Education reform and social change: Multicultural voices, struggles, and visions* (pp. 147–164). Mahwah, NJ: Lawrence Erlbaum Associates.

Oakes, J. (1985). *Keeping track: How schools structure inequality*. New Haven, CT: Yale University Press.

Ochoa, A., & Caballero-Allen, Y. (1988). Beyond the rhetoric of federal reports: Examining the conditions necessary for effective bilingual programs. *Equity & Excellence: The University of Massachusetts School of Education Quarterly 23* (4), 20–24.

Olsen, L. (1997). *Made in America: Immigrant students in our public schools*. New York: The New Press.

Padilla, A. (1990). Bilingual education: Issues and perspectives. In A. Padilla, H. Fairchild, & C. Valadez (Eds.), *Bilingual education: Issues and strategies* (pp. 15–25). London: Sage.

Pajares, M. F. (1992). Teachers' belief and educational research: Cleaning up a messy construct. *Review of Educational Research 62* (3), 307–332.

Peterson, R. (1995). What should children learn? A teacher looks at E. D. Hirsch. In D. Levine, R. Lowe, B. Peterson, & R. Tenorio (Eds.), *Rethinking schools: An agenda for change* (pp. 74–88). New York: The New Press.

Piaget, J. (1973). *To understand is to invent: The future of education*. New York: Grossman.

Pinar, W. (2000). Strange fruit: Race, sex and an autobiographics of alterity. In p. Trifonas, (Ed.), *Revolutionary pedagogies: Cultural politics, instituting education, and the discourse of theory* (pp. 30–46). New York: Routledge Falmer.

Pinar, W., Reynolds, W., Slattery, P., & Taubman, P. (1996). *Understanding curriculum: An introduction to the study of historical and contemporary curriculum discourses.* New York: Peter Lang Publishing.

Powell, R. (1999). *Literacy as a moral imperative: Facing the challenges of a pluralistic society.* New York: Rowman & Littlefield.

Quinn-Patton, M. (1990). *Qualitative evaluation and research methods* (2nd ed.). Newbury Park, CA: Sage.

Randoloph, C. H., & Everston, C. (1994). Images of management for learner centered classrooms. *Action in Teacher Education 16* (1), 55–63.

Ravitch, D. (1995). *The schools we deserve: Reflections on the educational crises of our times.* New York: Basic Books.

Richard-Amato, P. A. (1996). *Making it happen: Interaction in the second language classroom from theory to practice.* White Plains, NY: Addison-Wesley.

Richards, J. C., & Rodgers, T. S. (1997). *Approaches and methods in language teaching.* New York: Cambridge University Press.

Richardson, V. (1994). Teacher inquiry as professional staff development. *Teacher research and educational reform: The ninety-third yearbook of the National Society of the Study of Education* (pp. 186–203). Chicago, IL: University of Chicago Press.

Richey, R. C., & Nelson, W. A. (1996). Developmental research. In D. H. Jonassen (Ed.), *Handbook of research for educational communications and technology* (pp. 1213–1245). New York: Macmillan.

Riessman, F. (1976). *The inner-city child.* New York: Harper & Row.

Rippa, S. A. (1988). *Education in a free society: An American history* (6th ed.). White Plains, NY: Longman Press.

Rodriguez, L. (1995). Voice and empowerment: The struggle for poetic expression. In A. Darder (Ed.), *Culture and difference: Critical perspectives on the bicultural experience in the United States* (pp. 185–200). Westport, CT: Bergin & Garvey.

Routmann, R. (1994). *Invitations: Changing as teachers and learners K–12.* Portsmouth, NH: Heinemann.

Shannon, P. (1989). *Broken promises: Reading instruction in 20th-century America.* Granby, MA: Bergin & Garvey.

Shannon, P. (1990). *The struggle to continue: Progressive reading instruction in the United States.* Portsmouth, NH: Heinemann.

Shor, I. (1992). *Empowering education: Critical teaching for social change.* Chicago, IL: University of Chicago Press.

Smith, F. (1971). *Understanding reading.* New York: Holt, Rinehart, and Winston.

Snow, M. A. (Ed.). (2000). *Implementing the ESL standards for pre-K–12 students through teacher education.* Alexandria, VA: Teachers of English to Speakers of Other Languages.

Sleeter, C. S. (1996). *Multicultural education as social activism.* New York: State University of New York Press.

Stoller, P. (1977). The language planning activities of the U.S. Office of Bilingual Education. *Linguistics 11* (4), 45–60.

St. Pierre-Hirtle, J. (1996). Constructing a collaborative classroom. *Learning & Leading with Technology 23* (7), 19–21.

Street, B. V. (1984). *Literacy in theory and practice*. Cambridge: Cambridge University Press.

Stuckey, J. E. (1991). *Violence of literacy*. Portsmouth, NH: Boynton/Cook Publishers.

Taylor, D. (1998). *Beginning to read and the spin doctors of science: The political campaign to change American's mind about how children learn to read*. Urbana, IL: National Council of Teachers of English.

Walsh, C. (1996). Making a difference: Social vision, pedagogy, and real life. In C. Walsh (Ed.), *Education reform and social change: Multicultural voices, struggles, and visions* (pp. 223–239). Mahwah, NJ: Lawrence Erlbaum Associates.

Weaver, C. (1998). *Reconsidering a balanced approach to reading*. Urbana, IL: National Council of Teachers of English.

Weiler, K. (1988). *Women teaching for change: Gender, class & power*. Westport, CT: Bergin & Garvey.

Wells, C. G. (1981). *Learning through interaction: The study of language development*. New York: Cambridge University Press.

Wiese, A. M., & Garcia, E. (1998). The bilingual education act: Language minority students and equal educational opportunity. *Bilingual Research Journal 22* (1), 1–16.

Wiley, T. G. (1996). *Literacy and language diversity in the United States*. McHenry, IL: Center for Applied Linguistics and Delta Systems.

Williams, D., & Capizzi Snipper, G. (1990). *Literacy and bilingualism*. White Plains, NY: Longman.

Williams, R. (1983). *The year 2000*. New York: Pantheon Books.

Winterowd, W. R. (1989). *The culture and politics of literacy*. New York: Oxford University Press.

Yin, R. (1994). *Case study research: Design and method* (2nd ed.). Newbury Park, CA: Sage.

Yopp, K. (1992). Developing phonemic awareness in young children. *The Reading Teacher 45* (9), 696–703.

Index

Studies in the Postmodern Theory of Education

General Editors
Joe L. Kincheloe & Shirley R. Steinberg

Counterpoints publishes the most compelling and imaginative books being written in education today. Grounded on the theoretical advances in criticalism, feminism, and postmodernism in the last two decades of the twentieth century, Counterpoints engages the meaning of these innovations in various forms of educational expression. Committed to the proposition that theoretical literature should be accessible to a variety of audiences, the series insists that its authors avoid esoteric and jargonistic languages that transform educational scholarship into an elite discourse for the initiated. Scholarly work matters only to the degree it affects consciousness and practice at multiple sites. Counterpoints' editorial policy is based on these principles and the ability of scholars to break new ground, to open new conversations, to go where educators have never gone before.

For additional information about this series or for the submission of manuscripts, please contact:
Joe L. Kincheloe & Shirley R. Steinberg
c/o Peter Lang Publishing, Inc.
275 Seventh Avenue, 28th floor
New York, New York 10001

To order other books in this series, please contact our Customer Service Department:
(800) 770-LANG (within the U.S.)
(212) 647-7706 (outside the U.S.)
(212) 647-7707 FAX

Or browse online by series:
www.peterlangusa.com